Lavender Witchcraft

Crafting Queer Magical Practice

What people Are Saying About

Lavender Witchcraft

Extremely solid debut from Sam Wise that adds flavor & glitter to even the most well-rehearsed magical rituals. I absolutely loved it and you will too!
Cassandra Snow, editor of *Tarot in Other Words* and author of *Queering Your Craft* and *Queering the Tarot*

My first impression of this book was that I had stepped into a safe, welcoming space that was inclusive for all. Sam Wise, the author, makes some great points about the dearth of resources for fully queer-friendly spirituality and paganism, which is one of the reasons this book is such an essential read. Sam then lays the foundation with some queer history, showing that a lot of today's challenges aren't new at all — as too many members of the queer community know. From simple ways to bring queer energy into your working to understanding the roles of queer magic practitioners throughout history, this book is packed with methods for embracing magic and divinity without indulging heteronormative practices or beliefs.
I love the exploration of liminality as a crossover point between witchcraft and queer being. Witches are on the edge of things as are queer people, both experiencing "othering." As a queer, autistic witch, I relate to this deeply. As Sam says in the introduction, the metaphorical table everyone wants to be at needs to be bigger so more people can sit and be welcomed. This book takes an important step toward that goal, with one critical aspect being its secular nature; this witchcraft is not faith or path-specific, but describes practices anyone can enact. Truly, this volume has been an inspiration to embrace my own

identity more firmly and hold safe space for those who need it, however they identify or experience love — or magic.
Mabh Savage, author of *Practically Pagan: An Alternative Guide to Planet-Friendly Living* and *The Magic of Birds*

Sam Wise's *Lavender Witchcraft* serves as a helpful introduction for anyone first embarking on a Witchcraft path, or for those already established upon it who seek examples of how modern Witchcraft can be practiced outside of binary frameworks. This is something that is of benefit to all, regardless one's own identity. Wise's book is a breath of fresh air for readers within the LGBTQ+ community who yearn for a practice that is inclusive and cognizant of our sacred place in modern witchcraft and how our identities are reflected in the magical natural world around us. This book is also valuable for those outside of the LGBTQ+ community, highlighting important considerations that anyone in an intentionally inclusive community should be aware of. Sam Wise's *Lavender Witchcraft* is a very welcome addition to the Moon Books collection.
Olivia Church PhD, author of *Pagan Portals Isis, Sekhmet,* and *Osiris*

This volume is both an approachable introduction to queer Witchcraft and a love letter to queer Witches. As a queer Witch myself, I found myself affirmed throughout the book, and I also found myself thinking about new ways to continue queering my own practice. Sam Wise gives readers a little taste of everything — from recipes to astrology info to personal stories — and definitely whets the appetite for more exploration of the queerness of Witchcraft and the Witchiness of queerness.
Susan Harper, author of *Pagan Portals - Feminist Witchcraft*

Lavender Witchcraft

Crafting Queer Magical Practice

Sam Wise

MOON
BOOKS
London, UK
Washington, DC, USA

CollectiveInk

First published by Moon Books, 2026
Moon Books is an imprint of Collective Ink Ltd.,
Unit 11, Shepperton House, 89 Shepperton Road, London, N1 3DF
office@collectiveinkbooks.com
www.collectiveinkbooks.com
www.moon-books.net

For distributor details and how to order please visit the 'Ordering' section on our website.

ISBN: 978 1 917704 89 2
978 1 917704 88 5 (ebook)
Library of Congress Control Number: 2025939645

A CIP catalogue record for this book is available from the British Library.

Design: Lapiz Digital Services

UK: Printed and bound by CPI Group (UK) Ltd, Croydon, CR0 4YY
US: Printed and bound by Thomson-Shore, 7300 West Joy Road, Dexter, MI 48130

The manufacturer's authorised representative in the EU for product safety is:
eucomply OÜ - Pärnu mnt 139b-14, 11317 Tallinn, Estonia, hello@ eucompliancepartner.com, www.eucompliancepartner.com

Contents

Contents

This book is dedicated to every queer or questioning young person who feels lost or alone. I see you. I love you. I'm glad you're here.

Acknowledgements

This book would not exist without the support, guidance, and love of my community. Thank you from the bottom of my heart to everyone who shaped this work along the way. To my friends, teachers, and co-conspirators in Reclaiming and the Fellowship of Fire and Ice, for creating safe spaces for queer spirituality and for encouraging my growth as a witch and pagan. To the leaders of Berry College LISTEN for lovingly introducing me to queer culture and for showing me that we are stronger together. To all the author friends who patiently answered questions and gave advice about the traditional publishing process, and to Moon Books for helping bring this project to fruition. Thank you.

Thank you to Matt – my spouse, my anchor, my best friend. This book would not have been finished without your unwavering support, and it would not be as strong without your comments and feedback.

Thank you to Thomas for all of your love, patience, and encouragement, and for your help in rescuing stray dogs from conference center parking lots.

Above all else, thank you to the queer ancestors and living queer elders who inspired and guided this work. Thank you for fighting for our rights and freedoms. Thank you for your guidance and support. Thank you for building the communities I call home. I hope I've done your legacy justice.

Introduction

In June of 2022, I participated in my hometown's first public Pride celebration. It was a major turning point for our little town, nestled in the foothills of Appalachia and surrounded on all sides by politicians who ran on anti-LGBTQ+ platforms. We had received vocal support from local queer organizations, but we were worried about homophobic backlash. I was even more worried about backlash than the other organizers, and with good reason: I was going to be selling my books on witchcraft and offering tarot readings at the festival after the parade.

The parade and festival went well, and I was brought to tears multiple times by the outpouring of love and support from our community. This was the same town where I had been viciously bullied for my sexuality by classmates in school, but now I saw some of those same classmates bringing their children to the festival for rainbow face-painting and drag queen story time. It was a wonderful reminder that hate is a learned behavior and that love comes much more naturally.

I was also struck by how many people sought me out for tarot readings and spiritual advice during the festival. My reading style is very conversational, and through the tarot I was able to help people in my community plan for gender transitions, process grief over recent anti-LGBTQ+ legislation in nearby Florida, and more. I heard about people's struggles, triumphs, and fears for the future. Many of the people I did readings for asked me to recommend resources for developing their own queer-affirming spiritual practices.

At that Pride festival, while slinging cards next to an altar I had created to honor our queer ancestors, I realized how hungry my community was for safe, uplifting spiritual spaces. I was also pleasantly surprised by how many people showed an interest in witchcraft.

Many queer folks are attracted to witchcraft because of its DIY nature. There are very few rules to being a witch, and that makes it an accessible path for those of us who don't want our spiritual practice to be burdened by other people's biases. It's easy to see why the very fluid, personalized nature of witchcraft is appealing to our community.

And yet, the witchy crowd is not without biases or issues. Many witches put an emphasis on divine feminine and/or divine masculine energy and use gendered associations for the elements, which can be alienating for people who don't identify with a binary gender. An emphasis on sexual liberation and empowerment, while certainly healing for many witches, can make these spaces uncomfortable for asexual people. The toxic positivity culture that infects many spiritual spaces can add insult to injury for those of us who have been harmed by homophobia.

All too often, the burden of untangling these issues is placed on queer witches alone. We are told that this is how it has always been done, and that it is our responsibility to find ways to make it work for us. This can be exhausting, and it leads to many people giving up on finding safe, affirming spiritual communities.

In this book, I do a little of the untangling for you. My hope is that this will make it easier for other queer witches and our allies to create affirming traditions.

My goal is to show that moving away from problematic or outdated models does not take away from the power of our magic. Instead, our practice grows and flourishes as we find ways to lovingly engage with more diverse gender identities and sexualities. Instead of giving up our seat at the table, we build a bigger table so that everyone can comfortably be included.

Why Lavender Witchcraft?

Lavender (both the plant and the color) has been associated with the queer community since at least the 1920s. Before the rainbow became the universal symbol for queer pride, both lavender and the color pink were used by our queer ancestors to represent their identities and their fight for equal rights. In the 1920s, lavender began to be associated with gay men and lesbians. This association got stronger throughout the 1930s and 1940s.

When the United States government started a mass persecution of queer government employees in the 1950s, the queer community began to use lavender as a symbol of resistance and empowerment. This mass persecution has been named the Lavender Scare by modern historians who link it to the Red Scare, a persecution of suspected communists happening within the U.S. government at the same time. While the Red Scare is commonly taught as part of U.S. history, the Lavender Scare has been mostly forgotten outside the queer community.

In 1969, feminist leader Betty Friedan famously called lesbians a "lavender menace" and said that addressing queer women's issues would undermine the feminist movement. In response, a lesbian activist group disrupted the Second Congress to Unite Women in 1970, wearing lavender T-shirts with the words Lavender Menace printed on them. The activists took over the stage and opened a discussion about homophobia in the women's rights movement.

Even as the rainbow has become a more common symbol of queer pride, we can still see a connection between lavender and queerness in terms like "lavender marriage," which refers to a seemingly straight marriage between two people of opposite genders, one or both of whom is secretly queer.

This book's title, *Lavender Witchcraft,* honors the history of the queer community. It celebrates the way we have reclaimed the slurs and insults originally used to hurt us. It uplifts queer activism. It acknowledges that modern queer witches are part of a long lineage of queer spiritual seekers. We may be clad in rainbows, but we are standing on the shoulders of our lavender ancestors.

Lavender Magic Oil

Many queer witches, myself included, use lavender (the plant and the color) to represent queer identity in our rituals. I love working with lavender to call in queer ancestors, connect with queer deities, and celebrate my own identity.

One of my favorite ways to do this is with Lavender Magic Oil, a formula I created to help bring these energies into any spell or ritual.

To create this oil, you will need:

- One 4 ounce dropper bottle or other container.
- 4 ounces of a neutral base oil like olive, jojoba, or coconut.
- 40-50 drops of lavender essential oil.
- (Optional) 1 tbsp dried lavender buds. (Make sure to use dried, not fresh, because the moisture in fresh flowers can make your oil grow mold.)
- (Optional) 1 tsp purple luster dust or edible glitter.

To create this oil, start by adding the lavender essential oil to your container. If you are choosing to include the dried lavender and/or luster dust, add it now. Fill the rest of the container with your base oil and close it up. Once the container is tightly closed, gently shake it to combine the ingredients.

As you prepare the oil, focus on the way you plan to use it in your magical practice. Think about how you want to use this oil to celebrate your own identity and to call in queer energies to help you in your magic.

Accessibility Adjustment: If you are not able to mix your own oil blends, you can absolutely use a store bought product the same way in your practice. Lavender is a common scent in aromatherapy and is widely available. You can buy a lavender-scented massage oil, lotion, or bath salt and charge it with your intention to bring queer energy into your rituals.

Whom This Book Is For

This book is written for queer witches by a queer witch. This book is also intended to help allies who want to develop more welcoming practices. I use the word "queer" as an umbrella term for anyone and everyone who is not cisgender and straight. Cisgender means someone identifies with the gender they were assigned at birth. (For example, someone who was born a boy and now identifies as a man.) Straight means heterosexual – someone who is attracted only to the opposite gender. (For example, a woman attracted only to men.)

My definition of queer is intentionally very broad. I do not believe in gatekeeping. Everyone who is not cisgender and straight is welcome in my queer community. This includes transgender people, nonbinary people, asexual and aromantic people, and those who are still questioning their identity. It includes bisexual and pansexual people in straight-passing relationships. It includes people who use neopronouns (such as using xe/xem/xir instead of he/him/his or she/her/hers) and people whose identity does not fit a single label. Everyone has a place here.

I prefer to use "queer" instead of an acronym because I feel it is more inclusive. When we get hung up on acronyms, we often end up excluding some identities and/or putting pressure on people to identify with a label we approve of. We could try to add more and more letters to an acronym until all identities are included, but I find it easier to simply call ourselves the queer community. When I do use an acronym, I prefer LGBTQ+, which stands for lesbian, gay, bisexual, transgender, queer, and more.

Allies are also an important part of our community. While I encourage allies to learn about queer topics, it's important to keep queer lives and experiences at the center of these conversations. Instead of trying to be a spokesperson for the queer community, focus on uplifting and amplifying queer voices. Instead of trying to come in and fix things for us, ask us how you can help with the work we're already doing.

You do not need to be an expert on queer topics to read and understand this book. I try to avoid jargon as much as possible, and I try to define social justice terms as I use them. My goal is for this book to be accessible to all queer witches and their allies, regardless of their previous knowledge.

You don't need to be an expert on witchcraft to read this book, but you will probably get more out of it if you already have a solid understanding of the basics. This book is mostly focused on queer practices and doesn't cover many "Witchcraft 101" topics. If you are looking for a resource to help you master the basics, you may want to check out my previous book, *Witchcraft For Everyone.* Other beginner books I wholeheartedly recommend include *The Spiral Dance* by Starhawk, *A Witch's Guide to Spellcraft* by Althaea Sebastiani, and *Wild Witchcraft* by Rebecca Beyer.

You do not need to be any certain type of witch to read this book. This book focuses on *secular witchcraft,* i.e., witchcraft that is not part of any one tradition or religion, although I hope the discussions here will also be helpful for people within formal traditions looking to create more inclusive practices.

There is no right or wrong way to be queer, and there is no right or wrong way to be a witch. Below are just a few examples of what a queer witch's daily practice might look like:

- Connecting with nature by celebrating the cycle of the seasons, honoring the full moon with sacred rituals, and working magic inside a circle.
- Reviving the folk magic traditions of their ancestors, working with crossroads dirt and animal bones to cast spells, and reading the future with playing cards.
- Doing yoga, meditating daily, and working with stones or crystals.
- Building a practice of little acts of everyday magic, like blessing their morning coffee, enchanting cleaning products for spiritual cleansing, and doing tarot readings on the train ride to work.
- Connecting with ancient gods through shrines, offerings, and rituals.
- Combining magic with activism by casting spells as performance art, holding public healing rituals for marginalized communities, and working protection magic for protesters.
- And many, many, other practices that look completely different.

If you're anything like me, your practice probably includes a mix of all of the above. Or maybe it looks totally different from the examples on my list. Or maybe you're just starting out in your practice and aren't sure what it is going to look like yet. Wherever you are and whatever your practice looks like is just fine.

My goal in the following chapters is not to tell you how to practice. Instead, I want to share how I have queered my own magical practice so you can see what an inclusive practice might look like. Throughout the book, you will have opportunities to reflect on what you've learned and how you would like to apply it in your own life.

Chapter 1

Queerness and Liminality

Witchcraft thrives in the "in-between" and "outside" places that mainstream society often neglects. Witchcraft is the magic of individuals and small communities, not of institutions or occult societies. It is the magic of roots and dirt, blood and bone, moon and star. Witchcraft is hands-on, messy, and experimental. It is a political act. To be a witch is to be at home in liminal spaces.

Merriam-Webster lists two definitions for the word "liminal." The first is, "of, relating to, or situated at a sensory threshold: barely perceptible or capable of eliciting a response." The second is, "of, relating to, or being an intermediate state, phase, or condition." The word liminal comes from the Latin *limen*, meaning threshold. When we are in a liminal state, we are between two things. We are both, and we are neither. This both-neither state is deeply magical.

The liminal plays a big role in witchcraft, but queer identity is also very liminal. Queerness is marked as "other" by a society centered on cisgender, straight experiences, and queer people often find themselves pushed out of mainstream spaces. Especially in places where queerness is not accepted, queer people can certainly feel like they are "barely perceptible or capable of eliciting a response." And those of us who feel like our identities place us between traditional concepts of masculinity and femininity may find ourselves living in that magical both-neither space every day.

Queer spaces are liminal because they exist outside of the binaries of masculine/feminine. When we find ourselves unwelcome in the spaces available to us, we create our own special places between the worlds. Anyone who has attended a Pride parade or a drag show has probably noticed the electric, mystical energy in these spaces. Here, otherness is embraced and celebrated. Here, we embrace the Other as a reflection of the divine self.

Many gods, goddesses, and other divine spirits associated with the liminal also have a connection to queer communities. The Greek goddess Artemis, who is associated with lesbian love and defiance of traditional femininity, is the patroness of those who live outside of the established social order. The Norse god Loki is described with masculine pronouns, but he often appears in female form. The Fon *lwa* Legba and the Yoruba *orisha* Obatala are both masculine spirits with both male and female attributes.

Being comfortable with the liminal is an important part of witchcraft. Think about liminal spaces you encounter in your own life. What do these spaces feel like? How can you harness their magic in your practice?

Chapter 2

A History of Queer Witchcraft

For thousands of years, different cultures have connected queerness with magic. People who existed outside their culture's gender and sexuality norms were seen as keepers of sacred power. Today, we might identify these people as transgender, nonbinary, gay, lesbian, or some other modern label, but they had their own words to define their identities.

In Europe, Africa, Asia, and North and South America, many different cultures have connected magic and the Otherworld to people living outside of gender and sexuality norms. In some cases, these people were explicitly identified as witches, sorcerers, or magicians, while in other cases they were honored as healers, spiritual leaders, or prophets.

In their article, "Men-Women, Gatekeepers, and Fairy Mounds," Randy P. L. Conner says that, "people who leave behind traditional gender roles become bridges to the Other." For thousands of years, this idea has been at the core of queer spirituality.

Examples of queer ancestors who acted as spiritual guardians of their cultures include:

- Ancient Mesopotamian *sal-zikrum* (literally "women-men," transgender priests of the goddess Inanna).
- Ancient Roman *galli* (castrated priests of the goddess Cybele).
- Ancient Chinese *shih fu* (scholars and officials who often had same-sex relationships).
- Third gender spiritual leaders in indigenous North American communities, like the *Lhamana* of the Zuni nation, *baté* people of the Crow nation, and the *kwih-doh* of the Tewa nation.

Some of these queer ancestors had identities we would now classify as transgender or nonbinary, but not all of them. Many of them were associated with homosexuality or bisexuality in some way. Queer identity or, more accurately, social fears about queer people, have also informed folklore about witches and magic.

The witch as an archetype did not appear out of nowhere. Stories, art, and folklore about witches combine threads of older mythology about other, similar beings. Some of these stories go back to the very beginning of civilization. Many of these pre-witch stories are about women or feminine men who behave in ways that go against society's expectations based on their assigned gender. In many of these stories, the witchy figure is divine or supernatural.

Some of these figures, such as the Slavic Baba Yaga, rejected feminine gender roles in ways that can be read as queer. Some scholars describe Baba Yaga's pestle as a phallic object, giving her both male and female aspects. She lives in a hut in the woods and is said to kill and eat the men who stumble upon her home, but she is sometimes willing to help a brave, beautiful young woman. While Baba Yaga is never explicitly described as queer in Slavic folklore, it is easy to see how she is connected to negative stereotypes about queer women: she acts masculine, she hates men, and she is a "bad influence" on the young women she helps.

Queer men also play a role in shaping our ideas of witchcraft. In Iron Age Scandinavia, a *vitki* was a man who practiced the feminine magic known as *seiðr*. Men who practiced seiðr were seen as taking on a feminine social role, making them less manly. Even so, it was not uncommon for men to practice this magical art.

Heathen author and modern seiðr practitioner Cat Heath writes in her book *Elves, Witches & Gods* that:

> regardless of who was doing seiðr, there was always the implication of sexual deviance and promiscuity ... The association between magic and sexual deviance were preserved in Norwegian legal history well into the sixteenth century.

Even though seiðr was associated with sexual deviance, it was an important part of Norse society. Odin, the chief of the Norse gods, is a vitki.

When we talk about witchcraft, we're talking about magical practices from Europe, North Africa, and West Asia. But it's important to note that this connection between magic and gender nonconformity is also present in non-Western cultures. For example, in Yoruba mythology from West Africa, the orisha Oshun is associated with both magic and sex, and at least one legend describes her using her seductive charms on women.

This history is important for two reasons. First, it reminds us that queer people have always been here and have always been part of the history of witchcraft. Second, it can be a source of inspiration for modern queer witches as we create our own practices.

Chapter 3

Queering the Elements

In my queer, secular witchcraft practice, the two main groups of energies I work with are the elements and the planets. The elements are the forces that make up life on Earth, the building blocks of the world we live in. The planets are the forces that rule the heavens, and their movements affect our lives on Earth. These are the powers that shape the natural world.

Unlike deities or other spirits, the elements and the planets are not tied to any religion or belief system, which can make them feel safer and more approachable for those of us coming from religious trauma. Many queer people have had negative experiences with religion, and this can make it difficult to feel comfortable with anything that might be considered worship. Connecting with a god or goddess may not feel safe for someone who has been abused or oppressed in the name of someone else's gods. Because the elements and the planets are not worshiped, and because they are forces of nature rather than human-like spirits, they can be much less intimidating to call on in a ritual or spell.

Some people do not want to include spiritual beings in their practice at all, while others might want to believe but find it difficult to let go of their skeptical mindset. For these witches, the elements and the planets are a good place to begin because they are an observable part of the natural world. Connecting with these energies can help us feel like part of something greater than ourselves and can help us appreciate the wonders of nature, whatever our spiritual or religious beliefs might be.

There is a very old idea in witchcraft that "like attracts like." Each element and planet are associated with certain qualities and areas of life. If we want to increase or improve those areas in our lives, connecting more deeply with the associated element and/or planet can help us do that. For example, if I wanted to work on my self love, I might make an effort to connect with water, the element associated with emotions, love, and healing, and with Venus, the planet associated with love and beauty.

Modern witchcraft works with the four *classical elements* – earth, air, fire, and water – which were originally observed by the Ancient Greeks. Some witches also choose to work with a fifth element, called spirit or aether. The concept of aether as the fifth element was originally posed by Aristotle, and its association with the gods and the spirit dates back to Ancient Greece.

The elements are the basic building blocks of the natural world, and all of them must be present to make life possible. Take a moment to think about how each of these elements is present in your own body. Air is the element most literally present in our bodies, as we breathe it in and out all the time. Fire is in the electric impulses that fire our neurons and allow us to think and act. Water is in all of our bodily fluids, and the water in our cells. Earth is in our bones, providing structure and stability, and in the iron in our blood. If any one of these elements was absent, we could not exist.

Each of the four classical elements is associated with certain areas of human life. The four elements together make up a complete, balanced whole. That whole is associated with the fifth element, spirit. Each element is also associated with one of the cardinal directions. They also each have their own associated colors, symbols, and season.

Let's take a closer look at each of the elements.

Earth

Earth is the element of stability, growth, and permanency. It is heavy, patient, enduring, practical, nourishing, and community-oriented. Earth energy moves the most slowly out of all the elemental energies, but it often brings the most long-lasting results.

Earth is associated with the north in the Northern hemisphere and the south in the Southern hemisphere – whichever direction is associated with cold. Its season is winter. Its colors are warm-toned greens, black, gray, and brown.

Plants associated with earth include buckwheat, corn, honeysuckle, magnolia, mugwort, oats, patchouli, and vervain. Minerals, stones, and metals associated with this element include agate, brown jasper, green jasper, malachite, peridot, salt, emerald, and turquoise.

In magic, earth is associated with prosperity, success, physical health, financial gain, career goals, family, and commitment. Earth is associated with the pentacle, a pentagram inside a circle. It can also be represented with rocks or stones, coins, or live plants.

Many witches use salt to represent earth in their rituals. You could use any type of salt, but I like black salt because it enhances earth's protective and stable energy. Making your own black salt can be a wonderful way to connect with this element.

Making Black Salt

Black salt is used in witchcraft for protection, and to banish and repel unwanted influences. It's excellent for absorbing and neutralizing uncomfortable energy. You can make a batch of black salt for general protection, or you can make a batch to specially protect your queer community by adding ingredients you associate with queer identity.

Black salt is made by combining ordinary salt with other protective substances. It is traditionally made with iron scrapings, such as the scrapings from cast iron cookware, but many modern witches don't have access to iron scrapings in their daily lives. As an alternative, you can use ashes. (This is a great way to reuse ashes from incense!)

To create black salt, add equal parts table salt, iron scrapings, and/or ashes to a bowl. If you want to get a really strong black color, go ahead and add a bit of activated charcoal powder. This basic recipe works well for all-around protection.

If you want to create a more specialized black salt, you can include additional ingredients to support your intention. If you plan to use this black salt to get rid of unwanted energy or influences, include black pepper. (The kind you can buy at the grocery store works just fine.) If you'd like to enhance the stability and grounding aspects of the earth element in your black salt, you can also include dirt from the land your home is built on. And finally, if you'd like to use this black salt to protect your queer community or chosen family, include ground or powdered herbs associated with queer identity like lavender and/or violet.

Use your hands to mix these ingredients in a sunwise motion. *Sunwise* means moving in the direction of the sun, and is associated with blessings and with drawing things in. In the Northern hemisphere, sunwise is clockwise. In the Southern hemisphere, sunwise is counterclockwise.

As you mix your salt, think about the element of earth. Think about the stability of the ground beneath your feet and the protection of stone walls. These are the qualities of earth we are invoking in this spell.

Keep in mind that black salt is not edible. This is for external use only.

Accessibility Adjustment: If you don't have the energy or ability to mix up your own black salt, you can use a different type of "black salt" for a similar purpose. Black lava salt is a type of sea salt used in cooking, named for its dark color. You can substitute this for the more traditional black salt.

Air

Air is the element of the mind, the intellect, and abstract ideas. It is detached, changeable, mysterious, cerebral, creative, communication-oriented, and knowledgeable. Air energy moves the most quickly of all the elemental energies, but it doesn't always deliver lasting results.

Air is associated with the east in the Northern hemisphere and the west in the Southern hemisphere. Its season is spring. Its colors are yellow and gold.

Plants associated with air include almond, anise, bergamot, dandelion, lavender, lemongrass, and pine. Minerals, stones, and metals associated with this element include aventurine, citrine, mottled jasper, mica, and peridot.

In magic, air is associated with inspiration, intellectual pursuits, study, and communication. This is also the element that rules travel and technology. Air can be represented with a sword, knife, or other blade. It can also be represented with bells, chimes, fans, or feathers.

My personal favorite way to represent air in my rituals is with incense. The fragrant smoke that curls and dances as it rises is a perfect symbol of this element. Store-bought incense sticks or cones will work just fine for this. It can also be fun to make your own incense by blending dried herbs and resins for their scent and energy.

Blending Your Own Incense

Don't overthink your incense blends. You don't need a shelf with dozens of exotic herbs and resins. If you have a handful of common herbs and spices, you can mix and match them to bring the desired energy into your space.

Below are a few herbs to consider as you begin to create your own incense blends:

- Basil (associated with love, wealth, and protection).
- Cedar (associated with healing, cleansing, and protection).
- Cinnamon (associated with success, healing, power, love, and lust) [Note that cinnamon can be a respiratory

irritant. Always burn cinnamon in a well-ventilated space, preferably outdoors or in a room with open windows. Use cinnamon sparingly in your incense blends.]

- Clove (associated with protection, especially protection from gossip, and with love and money).
- Copal (associated with cleansing and love).
- Lavender (associated with love, happiness, peace, restfulness, and communication with the dead – also historically connected to the queer community).
- Nutmeg (associated with luck, physical health, and wealth).
- Pine (associated with healing, fertility, protection, cleansing, and abundance).
- Rosemary (associated with cleansing, protection, healing, exorcism, mental clarity, and love).
- Sage (associated with wisdom, the ancestors, long life, protection, and preservation). [Note that white sage, *Salvia apiana,* is endangered. Use common sage, *Salvia officinalis,* instead. They smell very similar when burned and have similar magical qualities.]

When you look at this list, you can begin to see how combining certain herbs together can strengthen the shared qualities of those herbs. For example, combining cedar with pine and rosemary will bring out the healing aspect of all three herbs. Likewise, combining cinnamon, clove, and nutmeg will bring out the wealth/money aspect of all three herbs.

To create your own incense blend, simply combine dried plant material and resin. To get a more consistent burn, grind your herbs and resins into small pieces or into a powder. Experiment with different ratios of each ingredient to see what you like best.

To burn this loose incense, you will need a fireproof container (cast iron works well) and a charcoal disk. Make sure you have charcoal specifically designed for incense, because the charcoal bricks used for grills contain chemicals that can be toxic when inhaled. You'll also want to make sure you buy charcoal that is labeled "self-igniting." You may want to invest in tongs to hold the charcoal when you light it so you don't burn yourself.

To burn your incense, begin by lighting your charcoal with a match or lighter. Hold the flame at a distance where it just barely touches the charcoal. If your charcoal is self-igniting, you should see small sparks when the flame catches. Wait for the charcoal to start smoking, then place it in your fireproof container. Sprinkle a pinch of your homemade incense on top. The incense will smolder on the charcoal, producing smoke.

Keep in mind that loose incense produces much more smoke than stick or cone incense, especially if your blend includes resins. Use a small amount at a time, and always start with less than you think you need.

Accessibility Adjustment: If you are unable to burn incense for whatever reason, diffusing essential oils works well as an alternative. The rising mist from the diffuser brings our attention to the element of air, just as incense smoke does. Just make sure you observe proper essential oil safety: only put 1-5 drops in your diffuser at a time, never run a diffuser continuously for more than an hour, and never apply an undiluted essential oil directly to your skin.

Fire

Fire is the element of transformation, illumination, and movement. It is passionate, strong-willed, and determined. Fire is associated with the south in the Northern hemisphere and the north in the Southern hemisphere – whichever direction is associated with heat. Its season is summer. Its colors are red and orange.

Plants associated with fire include cinnamon, clove, copal, cumin, chili pepper, ginger, nutmeg, and rosemary. Minerals, stones, and metals associated with this element include amber, bloodstone, carnelian, garnet, obsidian, red jasper, ruby, sulfur (warning: sulfur is toxic), tiger's eye, and any volcanic stone.

In magic, fire is associated with transformation, major change, courage, passion, sex, and adding energy to a situation. Fire can be represented with a wand or staff, but many witches use fire to represent itself by including candles in their spells.

Your candles don't need to be elaborate. A simple, unadorned white candle will get the job done. But some witches like to dress it up, personalizing their candles for the ritual at hand.

Dressing a Candle

Dressing a candle is the process of applying oils, dried herbs, and other substances to a candle before burning it. This is a popular method for casting spells, especially spells related to transformation or fast change.

Choose an unscented pillar or taper candle in a color that matches your intention. Use your intuition here – try not to rely too heavily on the lists of color correspondences you might find in books or online. If a color feels right to you, it is the right color to use. When in doubt, a white or undyed candle can be used for any purpose.

To begin dressing your candle, you'll need to coat it with a thin layer of oil. You can use any neutral oil that won't stain and doesn't have a strong smell. Olive oil is a good all-purpose option, but use whatever you have on hand.

If you happen to have essential oils on hand, you can incorporate them into the oil for dressing your candle. You don't need very much for this – one teaspoon of your neutral oil mixed with one drop of essential oil should be plenty.

To dress the candle, pour a small amount of oil into the palm of your hand. Rub your hands together, then use both hands to rub the oil into your candle. Starting with your hands at the middle of the candle, rub it up towards the wick and down towards the bottom of the candle.

Once your candle is all oiled up, take a moment to wipe off your hands.

Now you can add herbs or powders to the outside of the candle. Sprinkle your herbs carefully on the candle – they should stick to the oil. This infuses the candle with the energies of the herbs.

Choose your herbs based on the intended use for this candle. For example, if you plan to burn this candle to connect with the fire element, you might use fiery herbs like cinnamon, clove, and ginger.

Never leave a lit candle unattended. If you will be leaving the room where your candle is burning for more than a minute or two, snuff or blow out the candle and relight it when you return. If you have pets or small children, pay close attention and never leave them alone in a room with an open flame.

Accessibility Adjustment: If you don't have the energy or ability to dress your own candles, it is fine to get someone else to dress them for you. Another option is to simply sprinkle a ring of your herbs around the candle, or to sprinkle a pinch of herbs on top of a tealight. If you can't have open flames for any reason, use a flameless LED candle instead.

Water

The last classical element is water. Water is the element of emotion, empathy, and hidden mysteries. Water is associated with the west in the Northern hemisphere and with the east in the Southern hemisphere. Its season is autumn. Its colors are blue and cool-toned greens.

Plants associated with water include aloe, apple, catnip, coconut, elder, eucalyptus, lemon balm, passionflower, and any plants that grow in water, like lotus or seaweed. Minerals, stones, and metals associated with this element include amethyst, blue lace agate, coral, jade, lapis lazuli, moonstone, and seashells.

In magic, water is flexible, transformative (but in a gentler and more subtle way than fire), generous, healing, romantic, and always in motion.

Water can be represented with a cup or chalice, seashells, or ocean imagery, but it is most commonly used to represent itself in the form of a bowl or cup of water.

Making Floral Water

Water is the element of change and motion – because of this, it is often used to get stagnant energy moving. Water can also carry any intention you give to it, infusing whatever it washes with that energy.

This formula for a magic water using floral scents is inspired by Florida Water, a product that is widely used in North American folk magic. Florida Water isn't actually water – it's an alcohol-based cologne. I personally love working with Florida Water, but the high alcohol content dries out my skin and can irritate my eczema. This formula is truly water-based, so it is a gentler option. This formula also contains lavender and rose, two plants associated with queer identity and the queer community.

To make your own floral water, you will need:

- A vessel for your water, such as a jar or bottle.
- A pot for boiling water.
- A colander or sieve.
- 3 oranges.
- 1 lemon.
- 1 cup food grade rose petals.
- 1/2 cup dried lavender.
- 5 whole cloves.

- 1 cinnamon stick.
- 1 Tablespoon vodka or witch hazel (as a preservative).

Bring your water to a boil in a pot on the stove. While the water heats up, peel your oranges and lemon and slice the fruit into chunks. Once the water has reached a boil, add the oranges, lemon, rose petals, lavender, cloves, and cinnamon. Immediately turn the heat down to a simmer. Let the mix simmer for at least 30 minutes and up to two hours.

Strain out the herbs and transfer the water to your bottle or jar. Add the vodka/witch hazel and gently mix. This water will keep at room temperature for about a week, and for longer in the refrigerator.

You can use this floral water to prepare your space before a ritual or spell, or to cleanse your magical tools. You can sprinkle some over yourself whenever you feel like you need an energetic pick-me-up. To connect with the water element while gently uplifting your energy, add an entire batch of floral water to a hot bath and soak to your heart's content.

Accessibility Adjustment: If boiling water on the stove is not possible for you, you can make a version of this formula with essential oils, which is much faster. For this you'll need 1 tablespoon of vodka or witch hazel, 1 tablespoon of rosewater, 6 drops of sweet orange essential oil, 3 drops of lavender essential oil, 2 drops of clove essential oil, and 1 drop each of lemon and cinnamon essential oil. Add all of these ingredients to your water to create a lower-effort magic floral water.

Spirit

The fifth and final element is spirit. This is the most difficult element to define. The easiest way to describe spirit is as the sum of all the other elements together. Unlike the classical elements, spirit cannot be separated from the universe because, in some ways, spirit *is* the universe. If you've ever experienced the feeling of being part of something bigger than you, you have experienced this elusive fifth element.

The Emerald Tablet of Hermes Trismegistus, a foundational text in medieval alchemy, says that:

> As all things are derived from the One Only Thing, by the will and by the word of the One Only One who created it in His Mind, so all things owe their existence to this Unity by the order of Nature...

We could define spirit as the One Only Thing which all things are derived from, or as the Unity all things are ultimately a part of. Spirit exists beyond separation and labeling, and so it cannot be separated or labeled. Spirit is what unites all the other elements.

It is important to note that spirit is not God, or the Supreme Consciousness, or any other personified being. Like the other elements, it is an impersonal force. It's less like a god and more like the concept of the *Tao* or "The Way" in Taoism. The Tao is the natural order of the universe, but it is not the universe. The element of spirit is similar.

Spirit is the element associated with experiences that take us out of our bodies and make us feel like part of a bigger whole, like an ecstatic trance or a profound religious experience. Because spirit is less tangible than the four classical elements, it does not have any specific associations or symbols. You could represent spirit on your altar with things that bring up that feeling of unity, like photographs of galaxies or an antique item that has been in your family for generations.

Not every witch chooses to work with this fifth element. Some people prefer to keep their practices firmly grounded in the world they can see and feel, and that is absolutely okay. If all this talk of unity and out of body experiences isn't your thing, you might choose to stick to the four classical elements and leave spirit out of your practice altogether.

Gender and the Elements

Experienced witches may notice that I left out the traditional gender associations in my introduction to the elements. Frankly, this is because these gendered associations are too restrictive and can be alienating to people whose gender identity falls outside strict categories of male/masculine or female/feminine. It creates an unnecessary barrier, making it more difficult for trans and genderqueer witches to connect with the elements. It's high time we updated our way of thinking about gender in our magical practices.

The association of genders with the elements comes from medieval occult traditions such as alchemy and Hermetic magic. However, modern culture understands "male" and "female" very differently than the medieval occultists who created these associations.

In Hermeticism and alchemy, the universe is understood as a single whole (the Divine

Unity, the Source, the Prima Materia, etc.) divided into sets of opposites.

In his book, *Real Alchemy,* author and alchemist Robert Allen Bartlett says:

> One of the earliest observations of Nature was that everything has its opposite – day/night, male/female, hot/cold, wet/dry. The One divides into active and passive modes, with the active energy constituting the energies of life, and the passive one of the energy of matter.

In alchemy, the four classical elements are divided into *active* and *passive* classifications. Fire and air are considered active or volatile, while water and earth are considered passive or fixed.

Over the centuries, activeness has become associated with male or masculine genders and passiveness has become associated with female or feminine genders.

This may have more to say about our society's assumptions about men and women than it does about the elements. Medieval alchemists did not literally believe that earth is womanly or that fire is manly.

Even within medieval alchemy, some elements were seen as more active/masculine or more passive/feminine than others. According to Bartlett, fire is the most active ("masculine") element, while air is active, but less so than fire. Water and earth are both considered passive ("feminine") elements, but water is less passive than earth. Even when gender is being used as a metaphor, it has room for endless nuance and variation.

If you want, you can absolutely just ignore gendered associations in your magical practice. After all, "active" and "passive" are perfectly good descriptive words. If you don't feel the need to include gendered energies in your practice, that's totally fine!

For those who enjoy working with gendered energies, we can stay true to the traditional associations of the elements while also making room for more nuance and variety in gender identity and expression. We can honor masculine and feminine energies while also making space for energies that are nonbinary, genderfluid, agender, and more.

The gender associations I use for the elements in my practice are based on work done by my partner, who was inspired by medieval alchemy. He has given his permission for me to share and build on his model of the elements here.

In this model, earth is feminine because of its associations with nourishing, community building, and abundance. Earth is like a generous, nurturing mother. Fire is masculine because of its associations with movement, passion, and determination. Fire is like the father who protects his family and is a leader in his community. Air is traditionally seen as detached, changeable, and mysterious, so it is associated with agender and nonbinary identities and anyone who does not feel a strong attachment to any one gender. Water is traditionally seen as flexible and fluid and is the element of hidden mysteries, so it is associated with genderfluid and genderqueer identities and with anyone whose identity is fluid and defies an easy label.

This model works well for me, but feel free to switch it up if it doesn't work for you. You may associate the elements with different gender identities. Maybe you see fire as deeply feminine, or earth as nonbinary. That is perfect. Engage with these energies in a way that feels authentic to you.

My model is still very much informed by Western ideas of gender and gender roles, and non-Western witches will probably have different ideas about which traits are associated with which gender.

Some witches may feel like it's silly to project human gender categories onto the elements of nature, which is also entirely valid. I present my model not as something everyone has to follow, but as an example of one of many queer-affirming options for those who choose to relate to the elements in this way.

It's important to remember that no person is 100% masculine or feminine, and the same goes for the elements. Even though I consider fire a masculine element, I do still see feminine qualities in it, just like I see masculine qualities in the earth element.

Most of us are a mix of masculine and feminine traits, and most of us have deep connections to more than one element. For example, I am a woman who is very feminine-presenting, but I feel a strong connection to fire, which is traditionally seen as the most masculine element. I'm very strong-willed and passionate, which are fiery traits that are usually associated with masculinity in my culture. Most witches have similar experiences, which just goes to show how arbitrary our ideas of gender really are.

Chapter 4

Queering The Planets

The elements are the forces that shape life on Earth, but the universe is much bigger than our little planet. The celestial bodies we share a solar system with can also have a powerful effect on human life and can be powerful allies in magic and ritual.

There are ten "planets" that we typically work with in witchcraft. These are the Sun, the Moon, Mercury, Venus, Mars, Jupiter, Saturn, Uranus, Neptune, and Pluto. Of course, the sun and the moon are not planets, and Pluto is scientifically classified as a dwarf planet, not a true planet. But calling these celestial bodies "planets" is a little bit less of a mouthful than calling them "stars, planets, planetoids, and moons."

Of course, Earth is also a planet, but Earth is a much more constant presence in our lives than the sun, moon, and other planets, which may be closer or farther away from us depending on things like orbits and planetary rotation. We'll revisit Earth and the plants, animals, and other beings who call it home in the next chapter.

The Sun

The Sun is probably the celestial body with the most obvious impact on our day-to-day lives. After all, our planet's position around the sun is what causes the cycle of night and day and the cycle of the seasons. Without light and warmth from the sun, life on Earth would not be possible.

In Western astrology, the Sun, the Moon, Mercury, Venus, and Mars are called the *personal planets* because they are associated with personal identity and internal feelings and experiences.

The Sun rules the parts of our life that are most important to us – the things that are at the center of our life, like the sun is the center of the solar system. It is the planet of the ego and personal identity, of self-esteem and individuality, and of creative expression. The Sun is also associated with success and positive feelings.

In magic, the Sun can be called on for spells involving any of these qualities. If you want to explore your personal identity or express yourself in a more authentic way, the Sun's warmth and light can clear the way for you to do so. For queer people, the Sun is very much the planet of coming out and choosing to live as our authentic selves. The Sun can also be invoked for any spell where the desired outcome is success and/or happiness.

The Sun and Earth move in yearly and daily cycles, and the Sun's energy fluctuates throughout these cycles. The yearly cycle of the seasons is the focus of the Wheel of the Year, the holiday calendar followed by some witches, and will be covered in detail in Chapter 9.

We can also tap into the daily cycle of the Sun by observing the phases of the day: dawn, morning, noon, afternoon, and sunset.

Dawn, or sunrise, is when the sun first appears over the horizon. This is the ideal time of day for any magic related to new beginnings, fresh starts, or renewing old efforts that have grown stagnant. It is also an excellent time to work spells for change. For queer witches, dawn might be an especially appropriate time for a spell to give yourself the courage to come out of the closet.

Morning is when the sun is fully in the sky, but is not yet directly overhead. This is the best time of day for magic related to building on efforts you have already started. The morning sun is associated with growth and expansion in all areas of life. This would be an excellent time for spells related to finding queer community or becoming more confident in your identity.

Noon is when the sun is directly overhead in the sky. This is when the Sun's energy is at its strongest, and that strong solar energy can give a boost to any type of magic. This is also the best time of day for magic related to health, vitality, and strength.

Afternoon is when the sun is lowering in the sky, moving towards the horizon. The energy of the afternoon sun is ideal for finding clarity and resolution in situations that have become confusing or muddled. In this phase, the sun's rays cut through deception and illusion and help us to see things for what they really are. This is a wonderful time for spells related to navigating confusion or uncertainty around our identities, such as a spell to help sort out the complexities of gender identity.

Sunset is when the sun is moving below the horizon at the end of the day. This is the best time of day for magic to decrease or get rid of things. It is also a great time to simplify things that have become overly complicated and to tie up loose ends on projects that are nearly finished. For queer witches, sunset is a perfect time for spells to banish homophobia and transphobia from our lives.

If you want to connect with the Sun's energy, start by placing symbols of the Sun in your space. This could include actual images of the Sun, anything gold (both the color and the metal), and/or plants associated with the Sun such as sunflowers, marigolds, carnations, chamomile, rosemary, or bay leaves. You could also include the astrological symbol for the Sun (☉).

The Moon

The Moon is the planet associated with our inner emotional life. In astrology, the Moon rules our strongest emotional attachments and the things that make us feel safe, secure, and nurtured. It is the planet most connected to emotional expression, instinct, and intuition. This is also the planet that rules our daily habits.

The Moon doesn't actually make its own light. Instead, it reflects light from the Sun, which makes it look like the Moon is glowing to us on Earth. This concept of reflection is key to understanding lunar magic. The Moon helps us to reflect, turn inwards, and see ourselves clearly.

Astrology connects the Moon to motherhood, but this connection isn't limited to our literal mothers. The Moon is the Nurturer, and it rules all adults who take on a nurturing role for the children in their lives. The Moon is connected to all the ways in which parents make their children feel safe and give them room to grow.

The Moon also rules the ways we provide emotional nurturing for ourselves as adults. Many queer children and teenagers have to grow up too fast because of homophobia, transphobia, or other traumas. We may feel disconnected from our childhoods, or feel like our childhood ended too soon. The Moon can help us reconnect with our inner children, reclaim our childlike sense of wonder, and reparent ourselves.

Like the Sun, the Moon follows a cycle with several phases. One complete lunar cycle takes about one month – or 29½ days, to be exact. The changing appearance of the moon is caused by changes in the position of the Sun, Moon, and Earth around each other.

There are technically eight phases in the lunar cycle, but for the sake of our practice there are only four we need to worry about: the new moon, the waxing moon, the full moon, and the waning moon. Some witches also observe a fifth phase called the dark moon, which is technically part of the new moon phase.

The *new moon* is when only the tiniest sliver of the moon is visible – it almost looks like there is no moon in the sky. The key concept for this lunar phase is new beginnings. This is the ideal time for brainstorming, especially if you know you want a change but don't know exactly how to make it happen. This is the best time of month for spells and rituals to open up new opportunities or bless the beginning stages of a new project.

The *waxing moon* is the part of the lunar cycle when more and more of the moon is visible each night. The key concept for this phase is growth. Just as the moon appears to be growing in the sky, now is the time to grow the things you want to increase in your life. If you've finished your brainstorming, the waxing moon is the time to start taking action. This is the ideal time of month for magic to attract your desires into your life, whatever those things may be.

The *full moon* is when the entire disk of the moon is visible in the sky. The Moon's energy is most powerful during this phase. Because of this, the full moon gives an energy boost to any and all spells. The full moon is associated with fulfillment and completion, so this is a great time for a final push on something you've been working on. Some witches also find that they are more sensitive to energy at this time, so this is a great time to flex your physic abilities.

The *waning moon* is the part of the lunar cycle when less and less of the moon is visible each night. The key concept for this phase is downsizing. This is the time to get rid of things you don't want to hold on to, cut through confusion, and resolve conflicts. This is the best time of month for tying up loose ends both in your personal life and in your magic. Any spells to get rid of or simplify something will be more powerful during the waning moon.

Our fifth moon phase is the *dark moon*. Technically, the dark moon is actually part of the new moon phase. This is when the moon is not visible at all. Historically, this phase was associated with curses, hexes, and dark magic. The dark moon is still a powerful time for this type of magical dirty work if you are so inclined. Many modern witches are more likely to use the dark moon as a time for self-reflection, rest, and recharge.

The dark moon is a great time to take a brutally honest look at yourself and your life. Are you happy with who you are and how you live? If not, what do you need to change to create a life you can love?

If you want to connect with the Moon's energy, start by placing symbols of the Moon in your space. This could include actual images of the moon, art depicting the different moon phases, circular or oval mirrors, anything silver (both the color and the metal), and/or plants associated with the Moon such as aloe, coconut, eucalyptus, gardenia, passionflower, jasmine, lotus, or willow. You could also include the astrological symbol for the Moon (☽).

Timing Spells with the Sun and Moon

You probably noticed that the associations for different times of day overlap with the associations for the different moon phases. This means you can double up on your magical timing by choosing to cast a spell at the appropriate time of day and during the appropriate moon phase.

For example, let's say a witch who is questioning their gender or sexuality wants to cast a spell to help them find clarity in this area. This witch could choose to cast their spell during the waning moon, which is the moon phase associated with clearing out confusion. They could cast their spell during the full moon, because this is when the moon is brightest and can help "shine a light" on a murky situation. They could even choose to cast their spell during the new moon to help them open up to new possibilities. Which moon phase the witch chooses to work with depends on which approach they want to take with their spell.

Once they have chosen a moon phase to work with, our witch friend can double up on magical timing by also choosing an appropriate time of day for their spell. They could cast their spell in the afternoon to cut through the confusion and bring in a clear answer. They could cast their spell at dawn to welcome in their newfound identity. They could even cast their spell at sunset to banish any fears or doubts they may have about embracing their true identity.

Think of a goal or desire you would like magical help with. Is there a certain phase of the lunar cycle that compliments this goal? Is there a certain time of day that could lend power to a spell to achieve this? Think of how working with different parts of these cycles could help you approach this goal in different ways.

Timing our spells to align with the sun and moon is great, but it isn't always practical. Depending on your lifestyle, there may be certain times when you aren't able to do magical work.

Someone who works from nine o'clock to five o'clock probably won't be able to cast a spell in the morning, at noon, or in the afternoon. Someone with small children who need help getting up in the mornings and going to bed in the evenings probably won't be able to cast a spell at sunrise or sunset. Someone who is going to be traveling during the full moon probably won't have time to cast a spell during that moon phase. You get the idea.

Remember that the most effective spell is the one you cast. Special timing is optional. It's better to cast a spell at a time that works for you than to never cast it because you are waiting for the right moon phase. Your magic will still work, no matter when you cast it.

Be realistic with yourself about when you have time and energy for magic. Some witches do nearly all of their practice in the early mornings before work or school. Others work their craft late at night, after all the day's work is finished. Others squeeze magic in on lunch breaks, during their commute, and any other time they can fit it into their busy schedules. The best time for magic is the time that works for you.

The Sun, the Moon, and Gender

In modern Western culture, the Sun is often seen as masculine and the Moon is often seen as feminine. In Wicca, a neopagan religion, the fiery Sun is associated with the God while the watery Moon is associated with the Goddess. Many witches are also drawn to the twin Greek deities Apollo and Artemis, the god of the Sun and goddess of the Moon.

There's nothing wrong with working with the Sun and Moon this way if you find it meaningful, but it is important to remember that for every culture that sees the Sun as masculine and the Moon as feminine, there is another culture where the gender associations are reversed.

In Ancient Egypt, both gods and goddesses were associated with the Sun. Modern pop culture tells us that Ra and Horus are the main Egyptian solar gods, but we should remember that goddesses like Isis and Sekhmet also had solar associations. The moon, on the other hand, was connected to the masculine deities Khonsu and Thoth.

West African cultures typically worshiped a feminine sun deity and a masculine moon deity. For example, the Fon goddess Mawu is associated with the Sun, while her brother and husband Lisa is associated with the Moon. They are sometimes worshiped as one androgynous deity of Sun and Moon called Mawu-Lisa.

In the Japanese religion Shinto, the Sun is a goddess called Amaterasu, who is said to be the ruler of the heavens. The moon is her brother, a god named Tsukuyomi. In pre-Christian Germanic religions, the Sun was connected to a goddess named Sol or Sunna, while the Moon was connected to a god named Máni. Pre-Christian Celtic cultures seem to have seen the Sun as feminine, as we see in stories of solar goddesses like the Irish Áine and Grian.

I personally see both the Sun and Moon as having both masculine and feminine aspects, and whether I connect with them as masculine, feminine, both, or neither depends on what I need at the time. I encourage you to connect with these planets for yourself, read mythology about them from different cultures, and decide for yourself what, if any, gender associations fit your practice best.

Like with the elements, you don't have to work with gendered associations for the Sun and Moon if you don't want to. For some witches, seeing our own gender identities reflected in sacred stories can be affirming. For others, trying to fit human gender roles onto energies or forces of nature just muddies the waters. Neither approach is right or wrong. It is all about what works for you.

Queer witches often work with gender in ways that are different from heteronormative traditions. I know many queer witches who associate the Moon with transgender identities because it seems to change and transform throughout the lunar cycle. You might see the Moon as being masculine during the full moon, feminine during the new moon, and somewhere in between during other phases. You might see the Sun as nonbinary or agender. Feel free to experiment and see what feels affirming to you.

Mercury

After the Sun and Moon, the planet that probably has the most influence on our daily lives is Mercury. Our modern, urban, Internet-saturated lifestyle is full of Mercury energy.

Mercury is associated with communication, mental activities, intelligence, and reason. Mercury deals with how we gather information and interpret it to make sense of the world around us. It also deals with how we express ourselves by speaking, writing, and typing. It deals with transportation and travel and is sometimes connected to technology.

Any time you read a book, post on social media, commute to work, or Google something you're curious about, you are connecting with Mercury's energy.

Like all the planets in our solar system except Earth, Mercury is named after a Roman god. As witches who may at some point connect with both Mercury the planet and Mercury the god, we need to remember that the god and the planet are not the same. Making a point to keep them separate now will make things easier for you if you ever decide to connect with the deity down the road. This goes for the other planets and the gods they are named after as well.

Mercury is a wonderful magical ally for any and all work related to communication, learning, or transportation. If you want to get better at expressing your thoughts and feelings, connecting with Mercury's energy can help you.

For queer witches, Mercury can help us find the courage to fully express our gender and sexuality. This planet can also help us know when not to express our queerness. It's an unfortunate truth that not all places and people are safe for openly queer folks. Mercury can help us read the room and make a judgment call on how open we can safely be.

If you want to connect with Mercury's energy, start by placing symbols of Mercury in your space. This could include the color yellow, any items associated with communication or the exchange of information, and/or plants associated with Mercury like almond, bergamot, fennel, lavender, and lemongrass. You could also include the astrological symbol for Mercury (☿). The metal associated with Mercury is, of course, mercury, but this metal is toxic and is not recommended for use in your practice.

Venus

Venus is the planet of love, pleasure, and feeling good. Venus is not only connected to love and romance, but also to friendship and one-on-one partnerships of all kinds. This is the planet of art, beauty, and harmony. Some astrologers also connect Venus to money, although I personally do not resonate with this as much as the other qualities listed here.

Venus is your go-to planetary ally for all things related to intimate relationships. Whether you're looking to attract a new partner, make new friends, or strengthen an existing relationship, Venus can help. This is also the planet to call on when you create art or take action to make your life more beautiful. Self-love and simple pleasures also fall under Venus's domain.

I see Venus as an especially important ally for queer people and other marginalized folks, such as people of color and disabled people. Sometimes we can get so focused on safety and survival we forget to take time to enjoy our lives. Venus reminds us that we deserve to feel good and that simply taking pleasure in our lives as queer people is a revolutionary act.

If you want to connect with Venus's energy, start by placing symbols of Venus in your space. The traditional color for this planet is green, but many modern witches also connect Venus to pink because of its association with love and beauty. Venusian symbols for your altar could include either of these colors, any art that moves you (or art you've created!), tools used for grooming and self-care, copper, and/or plants associated with Venus like apple, blackberry, cardamom, daffodil, foxglove (be warned – foxglove is toxic if eaten!), hibiscus, hyacinth, and magnolia. You could also include the astrological symbol for Venus (♀).

Mars

Mars, Jupiter, and Saturn deal with all the ways we as individuals interact with society. As the last of our personal planets, Mars deals with our internal drives and how these drives push us to show up in the world.

Mars is the planet of energy, passion, ambition, and motivation. It is associated with both conflict and competition, and with courage. The flip side of this is that Mars also rules tension, anger, and acts of destruction – the ugly side of conflict. This is also the planet that rules sex.

If you struggle to be assertive or to stand up for yourself, Mars is the planet to go to for help. It is also the ideal planetary ally for spells to help you come out on top in a conflict or competition. And, of course, Mars is an important ally for all spells related to sex and sexuality.

If you find yourself in a situation with a lot of conflict, Mars can help you to armor up so you don't get battered. Many of us try not to seek out conflict, but most of us will find ourselves in the middle of a fight or disagreement at some point. Mars helps us to defend ourselves and our loved ones without escalating the conflict.

For queer witches, Mars can help us defend ourselves from bigots both inside and outside the LGBTQ+ community. Whether you're dealing with a homophobic acquaintance or with gatekeeping in queer spaces, Mars can help you protect yourself while seeking justice.

If you want to connect with Mars's energy, start by placing symbols of Mars in your space. This could include the color red, iron, images of shields and spears, and/or plants associated with Mars like allspice, cactus, chili peppers, garlic, ginger, and hawthorn. You could also include the astrological symbol for Mars (♂).

Jupiter

Jupiter is the planet of health, happiness, and good fortune. It is associated with wealth, power, and legal matters. This is also the planet that rules knowledge, especially lineages of knowledge and schools of philosophy. On a related note, Jupiter is the planet associated with religion and spiritual practice.

Jupiter is the "big picture" planet. While Mercury deals with everyday exchanges of information, Jupiter is the planet that deals with big pursuits of knowledge like going to university. While Venus deals with romantic partnership, getting legally married is a Jupiter move. While Neptune deals with our individual feelings of spirituality, all religious and spiritual institutions from the Catholic Church to a small yoga class are connected to Jupiter's energy.

In magic, you can call on Jupiter for any spell related to big life milestones. If you're looking to change careers, go back to school, get married, or move across the country, Jupiter brings a boost of good fortune to the transition. This is also the planet to call on for spells related to good luck, wealth, and abundance in all areas of life.

Jupiter can be a challenging planet for queer witches. This is the planet of authority and power, things that historically have not been on our community's side. I'm sure I'm not the only queer person who gets nervous about joining groups. When we've been burned by people in the past, the fear of being on the receiving end of more hate can make us isolate ourselves and blindly resist anyone who claims to have authority. If this is where you find yourself, Jupiter can help you find groups that are safe and supportive.

If you want to connect with Jupiter's energy, start by placing symbols of Jupiter in your space. This could include the color purple, tin, copies of important legal documents, images of money, and/or plants associated with Jupiter like anise, clove, chestnut, nutmeg, and sage. You could also include the astrological symbol for Jupiter (♃).

Saturn

Almost like a dark reflection of Jupiter, Saturn is the planet of diligence, self-control, and maturity – but also of limitations, obstacles, and difficult life lessons. Saturn is also connected to ideas of fate and family tradition.

Saturn gets a bad rap in astrology. Sometimes called the "greater malefic," this planet gets blamed for all kinds of misery. But Saturn isn't just the planet that makes bad things happen.

I prefer to think of Saturn as a force that tests things to see if they will last. Things that are built on strong, stable foundations stand the test of time, while things built on illusions or unhealthy patterns collapse under the pressure. Either way, we're left with greater wisdom and insight into the situation.

Saturn is connected to fatherhood, but like the Moon and motherhood, this isn't just about our dads. Saturn is the planet of discipline, and it rules the parts of parenthood that require us to discipline our children or help them understand difficult issues. As much as we'd love to always say yes to the kids in our care, sometimes as parents and mentors we have to tell them no or enforce a consequence when they break the rules. Saturn is connected to this concept of appropriate discipline, which is every bit as important as the Moon's nurturing.

In magic, Saturn can be invoked in spells to help develop greater self-control or stability. Saturn can also help us cut away excess baggage to make more room for what is really important. If you're going through a difficult transition right now, Saturn can comfort you with the knowledge that some things just aren't meant to last, and that doesn't mean anyone is at fault.

We talk about breaking generational cycles a lot in queer spaces. Many of us have inherited trauma passed down to us by our parents that we're ready to stop carrying with us. Saturn is the planet to call on for this necessary, difficult work.

If you want to connect with Saturn's energy, start by placing symbols of Saturn in your space. This could include the color black, the Saturn symbol (♄), thread or yarn to depict the threads of fate, animal bones, and/or plants associated with Saturn like elm, cannabis/hemp, ivy, mullein, skullcap, and yew. Saturn is also associated with poisonous plants like belladonna and datura, but I do not recommend these for inexperienced gardeners. Likewise Saturn's metal, lead, is toxic and probably shouldn't be included on your altar.

Saturn is the last of the *classical planets*, which are the planets that were known to the ancient Greeks and Romans. The other three planets in our solar system – Uranus, Neptune, and Pluto – weren't discovered until the modern era. Uranus was discovered in 1781, Neptune was discovered in 1846, and Pluto was discovered in 1930.

Because these planets (or at least human knowledge of them) are so new, there is less consensus about their personalities, rulership, and correspondences. We can't pull from ancient, medieval, and Renaissance sources, because these planets were unknown at that time. It's up to us to decide what these planets mean for us and how we want to represent them in our practices.

In this chapter, I offer some of my own suggestions for how to represent each of the modern planets on an altar, but I want to be very clear that these are based on my own intuition and research, not pulled from any historic source. If my way doesn't work for you, feel free to do something different.

Uranus

Uranus is the planet of freedom and revolution. Uranus is all about the unorthodox and unconventional – it's the planet of letting your freak flag fly. This is also the planet that deals with the future, scientific progress, and humanitarian movements. It also has a connection to friendship and community, and deals with group dynamics in general.

It's no secret that Uranus is the gayest planet. In fact, author Kris Brandt Riske explicitly connects Uranus to homosexuality in *Llewellyn's Complete Book of Astrology*. But more than that, Uranus is the planet associated with living unapologetically as yourself, even if it goes against what is expected of you.

Uranus is the planet of coming out of the closet and existing publicly as your true self, even if it scares you. It is the planet of experimenting with dressing and presenting in ways that are more gender-affirming. It is the planet of moving in with your polyamorous partners and openly living as a chosen family. Uranus is the planet most connected with authentically and unapologetically living your best queer life.

This is also the planet of protests and activism, and all other ways of actively doing the work to make the world better for everyone. I have two friends, both queer, who got legally married on the steps of a government building as part of a protest against anti-transgender laws. What a beautiful, kickass expression of Uranus energy in action!

In magic, Uranus can be called upon for the courage you need to fully express yourself in your queer identity. It can also be invoked to boost your activist efforts or strengthen your community. Call on Uranus when you feel alone in your weirdness and need help attracting a like-minded community.

If you want to connect with Uranus's energy, start by placing symbols of Uranus in your space. You could include the astrological symbol for Uranus (⛢). This is also the symbol for platinum, so platinum jewelry could also be used to represent Uranus.

I personally associate Uranus with light blue (the color of the actual planet) and with man-made crystals like opalite and bismuth. The plants I associate with Uranus are those that are stigmatized for their association with unconventional lifestyles, like wormwood (an ingredient in absinthe), THC-containing species of cannabis, and psychedelic mushrooms. I also associate this planet with stimulating plants like coffee, tea, and ginseng.

Neptune

Neptune is the planet of mystery, intuition, and the imagination. It rules idealism, spirituality, and all the ways we connect to a higher purpose. Neptune is also connected to dreams and psychic abilities, but it isn't all dreamy good vibes. Neptune is also the planet associated with illusions, lies, and addiction.

Sometimes escapism can be a good thing. Taking comfort in fiction can be a form of self-care. For example, sometimes we can get overwhelmed by the constant stream of news stories about the latest anti-LGBTQ+ crusade. When that happens, we can give ourselves some much needed comfort by watching, reading, or listening to a fictional world where queer people are safe, accepted, and loved. Escaping into a healthy fantasy for a few hours can help us return to a feeling of safety.

On the other hand, escapism can become addictive. We can become addicted to fictional escapism or to escaping into social media. We can also become addicted to using spirituality to escape our daily lives. This often shows up as *spiritual bypassing,* or using spiritual or religious concepts to avoid dealing with difficult situations or emotions.

Spiritual bypassing tells us that emotions like fear, grief, and anger are sinful, demonic, or low-vibrational and must be avoided at all costs. This can also show up as using spiritual practices like meditation or prayer to shut down difficult thoughts and emotions.

Extreme escapism and spiritual bypassing can only make us feel worse, because they keep us from processing our difficult feelings.

Despite all this, Neptune is one of my favorite planets. Maybe it's because I was born in the hour of Pisces, the dreamy zodiac sign ruled by Neptune, but I love the mystical energy of this planet. Neptune reminds us that we are magical beings made of star stuff and helps us to appreciate the mysteries of the universe.

In magic, Neptune is wonderful in spells for strengthening psychic abilities or spiritual connections. If you would like to feel more connected to the spiritual world but have a hard time turning off your inner critic, connecting with Neptune's energy can help you open up to spiritual experiences. Neptune can also be invoked for a boost in creativity or for artistic inspiration.

If you want to connect with Neptune's energy, start by placing symbols of Neptune in your space. You could start with the astrological symbol for Neptune (♆).

I personally associate this planet with deep blue (the color of the actual planet), images of the night sky and the ocean, and night-blooming flowers like moonflower, jasmine, and flowering tobacco. The plants I associate with Neptune are those that have sedative properties or promote vivid dreams, like valerian, mugwort, lavender, and passionflower.

Pluto

Pluto may no longer be scientifically classified as a planet, but it still plays an important role in modern astrology. Pluto is the planet of death and rebirth. Pluto's energy is like a forest fire, burning away dead material to clear the way for new growth. Pluto is associated with destruction and regeneration. Above all, it is the planet of transformation.

Pluto is the planet to work with when you are navigating a major transition, ending a cycle, or grieving something lost. Pluto helps us acknowledge that death (both literal and metaphorical) is painful, and it helps us make space for that pain, process it, and eventually move through it.

Pluto is also a powerful energy to call on when you need to end something. If you know you need to break up with your partner but have been putting it off, Pluto can help you find the strength to finally make a clean break. If you know you need to move out of your parents' home because they aren't supportive of your identity, Pluto can help you finally leave the nest. If your current job isn't accepting of your gender identity, Pluto can help you get your affairs in order so you can quit with grace.

Because of its association with transformation, Pluto can also be invoked during a gender transition. Whether you're just starting to dress in a more affirming way, just started hormone replacement therapy, or are about to change your legal name and gender, you are operating firmly within Pluto's domain. While Uranus deals with experimenting with your gender and trying out new labels, Pluto is all about finally finding a gender expression that feels authentic and settling into that new identity.

Invoke Pluto when you need a major change, or when a major change has recently happened and you need help processing it. Pluto is all about shaking things up and transforming our lives, often in ways we didn't expect. When you work with Pluto in a spell, don't be surprised if the results aren't exactly what you expected.

If you want to connect with Pluto's energy, start by placing symbols of Pluto in your space. You could start with the astrological symbol for Pluto (♇).

I personally associate this planet with the color gray, with images of snakes and snakeskin, and with glass, obsidian, and other materials created through extreme heat. Instead of associating Pluto with a plant, I associate it with mushrooms and other fungi, which do the important work of breaking down dead organic material.

Brewing a Planetary Essence

My favorite way to incorporate the energy of the planets into my daily life is with these essences. By bottling up the energy of a specific planet, you can invoke that planet whenever you need its assistance. You could add a few drops of your essence to a bath spell, use it to anoint a candle (carefully and using only a little bit, because these are flammable), or sprinkle it over the tools you use in your magic.

Because we are using food-safe ingredients, you can even add these essences to your food or drink to physically take on the energy of a planet. You can add a few drops to your morning coffee, a cup of tea, or a glass of water and drink it to help you embody the qualities of your chosen planet.

Remember to be mindful of food allergies and sensitivities if you plan to eat or drink this essence. Never ingest anything that might give you an allergic reaction or make you sick. If in doubt, only work with the essence externally. If you do decide to add the essence to your food or drink, only use a few drops at a time.

To make a planetary essence, you will need:

- A jar or other container.
- Between 3 and 7 food-safe dried herbs associated with the planet of your choice (refer to the chart below for herbs and numbers associated with each planet).

- Clear liquor like vodka, rum, or similar.
- A piece of paper.
- A pen, pencil, or marker in a color associated with the planet of your choice (see the chart below for color correspondences).
- (Optional) a stone or metal associated with the planet of your choice.
- A container to store your finished essence in. (I like tincture bottles with glass droppers, but use what you have on hand.)

These essences are made with a very simple infusion process. Start by filling your clean jar with the food-safe herbs you have chosen. You don't need a lot of plant matter, because this isn't a medicinal tincture. What matters is the energy of the plants. A tablespoon of each herb will be more than enough.

I recommend working with dry herbs to avoid any potential issues with mold or spoiled plant matter. You also want to make sure the herbs you use are food-safe. The best way to guarantee food-safe dried herbs is to buy them from a grocery store, herb shop, or other reputable vendor. If you grow or forage the plants yourself, do your research and make sure you are 100% certain they are safe to eat. If you forage for plants, make sure you have a positive ID from an experienced forager before eating them – do not rely on apps or AI foraging software, which are not reliable.

Once you have added all your herbs to the jar, simply fill it to the top with your clear liquor (or liquor substitute; see the accessibility adjustment below). Close up the jar and set it aside for a moment.

Take out your paper and pen and draw the astrological symbol for the planet you are working with. You can find the symbols listed earlier in this chapter, or in the chart below for your convenience. Once the ink has dried, place the jar on top of the paper – if you will be moving your jar around or are concerned that it will get knocked over, tape the paper to the bottom of the jar with the symbol facing into the jar of essence.

If you want to, you can also get a small piece of metal associated with the planet you are working with (like copper pennies for Venus or silver jewelry for the Moon) and place it around or on top of your jar. You can also do this with stones associated with the planet.

You may want to speak a few words at this point. You could say something like, "I ask that this liquid be infused with the energy of [planet], so that I might use it to connect with this celestial ally."

Place your jar in an out-of-the-way place for several days. I like to infuse my essences for a number of days associated with the planet I'm working with. For example, if I am making a Jupiter essence, I will infuse it for six days, because six is the number associated with Jupiter.

After several days, open your jar and strain the solid plant material out of your essence. You should be left with a clear liquid, which may have taken on a slight color and smell from the herbs. Store this liquid in the container of your choice.

I recommend labeling your essence so you remember which planet it is connected to. I label my essences with the astrological symbol of the planet. You can use a permanent marker to write or draw a label on your container, or you can make an easy DIY label by taping a piece of paper to the container.

Accessibility Adjustment: If you cannot use alcohol for any reason, you can infuse your herbs in water instead. Just be aware that this essence will be less shelf-stable than the version with alcohol, so it will need to be stored in the refrigerator.

Planetary Correspondences

Planet	Number(s)	Color(s)	Plants	Metals + Stones
Sun (☉)	1	Gold	Bay leaves, carnations, chamomile, marigold, rosemary, sunflowers	Amber, carnelian, diamond, gold, sunstone, tiger's eye, topaz
Moon (??)	2	Silver	Aloe, coconut, gardenia, jasmine, lotus, passionflower, willow	Aquamarine, clear quartz, moonstone, pearl, selenite, silver
Mercury (☿)	3	Yellow	Almond, bergamot, fennel, lavender, lemongrass	Aventurine, mottled jasper, mica
Venus (♀)	4	Green (traditional), pink (modern)	Apple, blackberry, cardamom, hibiscus, hyacinth, magnolia	Copper, coral, green jasper, jade, lapis lazuli, malachite, turquoise
Mars (♂)	5	Red	Allspice, cactus, chili peppers, garlic, ginger, hawthorn	Bloodstone, carnelian, garnet, iron, onyx, red jasper, ruby
Jupiter (♃)	6	Purple	Anise, clove, chestnut, nutmeg, sage	Amethyst, sugilite, tin
Saturn (♄)	7	Black	Cannabis, elm, mullein, skullcap	Brown jasper, hematite, jet, obsidian, onyx
Uranus (⛢)	8	Light blue	Coffee, ginseng, tea, wormwood	Bismuth, opalite, platinum
Neptune (♆)	9	Deep blue	Jasmine, lavender, mugwort, passionflower, valerian	Amethyst, turquoise
Pluto (♇)	10	Gray	All mushrooms	Glass, obsidian

Chapter 5

Rooting Down with Queer Nature Magic

We've spent plenty of time with the planets that share our solar system, but now it is time to turn our attention to the ground beneath our feet. In this chapter, we will talk about Earth, the many creatures who call this planet home, and how connecting with the natural world can be a source of power for queer witches.

You may see both witchcraft and paganism lumped together under the label of "earth-centered religions" or "nature worship." While not all witches connect to nature in the same way, most witches draw power from nature and feel that the natural world is sacred.

These labels are also sometimes used for indigenous North American spirituality, African Traditional Religions, and several other spiritual paths that include reverence for the natural world. The term "nature worship" can be misleading.

Those of us coming from a Western background have an understanding of worship that is shaped by Western religions, especially Christianity. For many of us, the word "worship" conjures images of quiet churches, solemn chanting or prayers, and lives spent in the service of a distant god. We see worship as a giving away of ourselves in the service of a higher power.

Nature worship does not mean serving something greater than us. Nature worship is a recognition of mutual importance and connection. In earth-centered traditions, we recognize that non-human beings such as animals, trees, plants, and fungi are an important part of the physical and spiritual world, just as humans are.

Instead of a spiritual hierarchy that places humans above the natural world and a god above humans, earth-centered traditions embrace a complex web of relationships between equals. This sacred web is the essence of nature worship.

Naturalist, ecophilosopher, and author Lyandra Lynn Haupt beautifully describes this worldview in her book, *Rooted: Life at the Crossroads of Science, Nature, and Spirit:*

> Our bodies, our thoughts, our minds, our spirits are affected by the whole of the earthen community, and affect this whole in return. This is both a mystical sensibility and a scientific fact. It is an awareness that makes us tingle with its responsibility, its beauty, its poetry. It makes our lives our most foundational form of activism. It means everything we do matters, and matters wondrously.

Humanity is an essential part of the natural world – but so is every other species. This balance of resources and relationships is the oldest and strongest magic. As witches, all of our rituals and spells draw from the ancient power of this sacred web.

My favorite description of magic comes from an author who, as far as I know, did not identify as a magician. Ursula K. Le Guin may not have been a witch, but she simply and eloquently explains the connection between nature and magic in her novel *A Wizard of Earthsea*:

> It is no secret. All power is one in source and end, I think. Years and distances, stars and candles, water and wind and wizardry, the craft in a man's hand and the wisdom in a tree's root: they all arise together. My name, and yours, and the true name of the sun, or a spring of water, or an unborn child, all are syllables of the great word that is very slowly spoken by the shining of the stars. There is no other power. No other name.

Mindfulness of our place in the world and our connections to other beings is one of the most important parts of witchcraft, and I firmly believe that this awareness is what separates a novice from an advanced witch. Nature worship – whatever that might look like for you – evolves naturally from a healthy witchcraft practice.

This reverence for nature is sometimes connected to a concept called *animism*. Merriam-Webster defines animism as

> 1: a doctrine that the vital principle of organic development is immaterial spirit, 2: attribution of conscious life to objects in and phenomena of nature or to inanimate objects, and 3: belief in the existence of spirits separable from bodies.

These definitions are clunky and can make it sound like animists believe every tree and stone has a human-ish intelligence. This is not the case. Author and philosopher Emma Restall Orr gives a better definition of animism in her book, *The Wakeful World: Animism, Mind, and the Self in Nature*. Orr argues that animism is:

> based upon the idea that mind and matter are not distinct and separate substances, but an integrated reality, rooted in nature.

To an animist, the natural and the spiritual are one and the same. The mundane is sacred. This idea is at the very core of most witchcraft traditions.

Most of us can tell that a tree is not intelligent in the way a human is intelligent – but does that mean the tree isn't intelligent at all? Is it possible that our definition of intelligence, which requires human-like behavior, is too narrow? What if we seriously considered that there are non-human beings that are just as complex and self-aware as we are?

Trees are one of my favorite examples of non-human intelligence. When we look at a tree, we see an unmoving being and assume that this is the full picture. But research has revealed that trees have a complex inner life.

As Potawatomi ecologist Robin Wall Kimmerer points out in her book *Braiding Sweetgrass: Indigenous Wisdom, Scientific Knowledge, and the Teachings of Plants*:

> There is now compelling evidence that our elders were right – the trees are talking to one another. They communicate via pheromones, hormonelike compounds that are wafted onto the breeze, laden with meaning.

Trees also communicate and share resources via the network of mycelia (the "nervous system" of mushrooms and other fungi) that runs between their roots, connecting one tree to another. Trees pass messages into the fungus, which carries these messages to nearby trees.

We also know that trees are capable of feeling pain and possibly even something like our own emotions.

As Haupt says in *Rooted*:

> We know that beeches, spruce, oaks, and certainly myriad other species yet unstudied, register a version of pain – not human pain or dog pain, but tree pain. When an insect or caterpillar bites a leaf, electrical signals are released by the foliage tissue, mirroring the response of injured human tissue.

Haupt also notes that:

> Neurotransmitters that we typically associate only with the demands of human life are found in trees and other plants: dopamine (in humans, it regulates emotional

response and feelings of physical and emotional wellbeing), serotonin (mood and social behavior), and glutamate (communication between nerves, learning, memory).

What other hidden intelligences are we overlooking? Both witchcraft and animism ask us to consider these non-human intelligences and to be mindful of our own relationships with them.

For queer people who want to deepen their spiritual practice but aren't sure where to start, I always recommend starting with the natural world. Nature is accepting and nurturing. It does not judge or preach or demand perfection. Nature is messy, and it gives us permission to be messy in how we connect with it. For those of us who are used to judgment from the people around us, this can be deeply healing.

We are all surrounded by the natural world at all times, in all places. There is not a single human alive who is not constantly in touch with nature, whether they live in a mountain cabin or in an apartment in the big city. Even astronauts who have left our planet are still surrounded by the strange and beautiful nature of space. We are never disconnected from the web, because the web is everything.

Instead of going to a park or natural wonder to connect with nature, I encourage you to focus on connecting with the parts of the natural world you already interact with every day.

When you feed your cat or water your houseplants, take a moment to feel grateful for these connections across species. When you eat an apple, feel grateful for the tree that grew the fruit, the sun and water that nourished it, the fungus and bacteria that live in symbiosis with the tree, and the human hands that picked the apple and transported it to you. When you walk from your front door to your car, think about the dozens of plants, insects, bacteria, and fungus coexisting in the ground under your feet, even beneath the asphalt. This is everyday nature worship.

As you practice being more mindful of your relationships with the natural world, you may find yourself drawn to specific locations, animals, plants, and other allies. Maybe you have a favorite animal that you feel a special connection to. Maybe there is a specific tree you pass on your way to work every day that always lifts your mood. Maybe you live in an urban area and feel a deep connection to the city itself. These animals, plants, and locations can be your spiritual allies. Leaning into these relationships is a wonderful way to deepen your spiritual practice.

In *Braiding Sweetgrass*, Kimmerer discusses the relationship between humans and sweetgrass plants. She writes about one of her graduate students, who created an experiment to study the effects of different harvesting methods on sweetgrass plants. The results were unexpected.

Kimmerer writes:.

> The surprise was that the failing plots were not the harvested ones, as predicted, but the unharvested controls.

She offers the following explanation of this surprising outcome:

> The sweetgrass that had not been picked or disturbed in any way was choked with dead stems while the harvested plots were thriving. Even though half of all stems had been harvested each year, they quickly grew back, completely replacing everything that had been gathered, in fact producing more shoots than were present before harvest. Picking sweetgrass seemed to actually stimulate growth.

Kimmerer theorizes that over its many centuries of use by indigenous North American cultures, sweetgrass has become dependent on humans to create just enough disturbance to stimulate increased growth. She describes this relationship as a *symbiosis*, a mutually beneficial relationship between two species.

For sweetgrass and some other plants that have evolved alongside humans, sustainable harvesting actually leads to healthier plants. The plants give to us and we give back to them. We work with the plant in a mutually beneficial relationship.

We can invoke this same type of relationship in our magical practices. Maybe you don't have the means to harvest your own plants, but you can still express gratitude for the plants you use. When possible, you can purchase from suppliers who use sustainable harvesting practices. At the very least, you can act with respect for the plants, animals, and other creatures you benefit from.

In witchcraft, this means viewing each being we include in a spell as a partner in our magic. In my personal practice, I do this by speaking directly to them, explaining what I am asking of them in this spell, and thanking them for their assistance. For example, if I work with roses in a love spell, I might say something like, "Roses, I ask you to help me bring a sense of love and romance into my life. Thank you for your help." You may find that this works for you, or you might develop your own ways of respectfully acknowledging your partners in magic.

The goal of nature worship is to create genuine relationships with non-human beings. When we lean into this practice, we go from using roses in a love spell because we read somewhere that roses are associated with love, to lovingly calling on our friend and ally, the rose plant, to work together to bring love into our lives. This makes for deeper and more powerful magic.

Introducing Yourself to Non-Human Neighbors

If you are new to nature worship or to working magic in this way, this exercise will help you to start thinking about the non-human beings around you as important parts of your community.

Take a walk through the outdoor area immediately outside your home. The pace of your walk should be slow and relaxed. Feel free to listen to your favorite meditation music as you walk.

If you want to and feel comfortable doing so, you might do this walk barefoot – just be careful not to hurt your feet! Urban areas are not always safe places for bare feet, especially in the summer when asphalt can get uncomfortably hot. However, if it is safe to go shoeless (if there is lots of nice, soft grass, for example), that can be a great way to connect directly with the ecosystem.

Walk slowly through the area and stop every time you see a new plant, animal, tree, or stone.

Either out loud or in your head, greet each new neighbor as you notice them. You can say something like, "Hello, daffodils," or "Nice to see you, dragonfly."

If you don't know the name of a neighbor's species, you can greet them with a description instead. For example, you might say, "Hello, green plant with tiny purple flowers."

Feel free to reach out and touch the plants as you greet them – just be wary of species that cause skin irritation, like poison ivy or stinging nettle! Pay attention to how the leaves or blades of grass feel under your fingertips. Touch the plant affectionately, like you would a friend.

You can use the same friendly touch for trees and stones, but it's best to greet insects and animals from a comfortable distance so you don't startle them.

As you walk, make a list of all the species you meet. (You can do this as a note on your phone, or bring a small notepad if you want this to be an unplugged activity.) This will help you start to learn and remember who your non-human neighbors are.

When you don't know the species of a plant or animal, take a picture or write down a description. Once you've finished your walk, you can do some research and see if you can identify this species so you'll know for next time.

You can identify types of rocks the same way you would identify a plant or animal species. For example, I live in an area that naturally has a lot of quartz and some mica, but there is also a lot of granite gravel in my neighborhood that has been brought in for landscaping.

As you walk, try to notice if you feel strongly attracted to any specific plants, trees, animals, or stones. Those neighbors might be a good choice if you want to work more closely with an ally in the natural world.

When you've finished your walk and have a good list, leave a small gift for the local nature spirits as a sign of your thanks and your commitment to being a good neighbor.

Good choices for offerings include fresh water, unsalted nuts and seeds, and fresh fruit. Whatever you leave, make sure it is biodegradable and won't harm any local animals that might snack on it!

Accessibility Adjustments: If walking is difficult for you, you can absolutely use a mobility aid or ask someone to help you. Another alternative is to do this exercise sitting down outdoors. You can do this exercise sitting on your front porch, or on a park bench, or on a picnic blanket on the ground. Instead of touching plants, you can simply greet them by waving to them from a distance.

If it is not safe for you to walk alone in the area around your home, do not do so. If you would feel safe walking with another person, see if you can find a friend to go with you. If this isn't possible, you might try doing this exercise in a place that feels safer, like a library, park, or other public area. And finally, if you don't have transportation to a safer area, you can do this exercise indoors, standing at a window and greeting the non-human beings you see outside from a distance.

Nature Worship Is Queer-Affirming

Nature worship opens our eyes to the everyday magic of the world we live in, but it changes us in other ways as well. When we accept the basic premise that what is natural is holy, it reframes how we view our own identities and actions. This can be deeply healing for queer people, especially those who have been told that being queer is unnatural or unclean. When we look to other species, we quickly realize this just isn't true.

Nature is queer and to be queer is natural. Social scientists and feminist scholars have been arguing for decades that identity markers like race, gender, and sexual orientation are social constructs (ideas or concepts created as a product of culture) and are not actually rooted in pure biological fact. And these days, many biologists seem to agree.

Let's look at biological sex as an example. How many biological sexes naturally occur in the human species? Two? Not exactly.

Writing for *Scientific American*, journalist Claire Ainsworth points out that biological sex in humans isn't as cut and dry as male vs. female. Up to 1% of humans are *intersex*, meaning they have a mix of traits traditionally considered "male" and "female." But even in people who are not intersex, biological sex can be less straightforward than we might think.

Ainsworth writes:

> When genetics is taken into consideration, the boundary between the sexes becomes even blurrier.

Later in the article, they go on to say:

> Scientists have identified many of the genes involved in the main forms of [intersex conditions], and have uncovered variations in these genes that have subtle effects on a person's anatomical or physiological sex. What's more, new technologies in DNA sequencing and cell biology are revealing that almost everyone is, to varying degrees, a patchwork of genetically distinct cells, some with a sex that might not match that of the rest of their body.

Humans are not the only species with this kind of diversity in biological sex. Clown fish are known for their ability to change their sex (usually from male to female when there is a shortage of reproducing females), but many other types of fish and some reptiles also change their sex in response to their environment.

Some birds, such as cardinals, parrots, and chickens, can be born with a condition called *bilateral gynandromorphism,* which means they are literally half male and half female, with one side of the body being biologically male and the other being biologically female. Bilateral gynandromorphism is also found in other species, including reptiles and insects.

Outside of the animal kingdom, sex is even less binary. Botanists have identified three sexes in flowering plants: male, female, and "perfect" flowers, which contain both male and female anatomy. Some species of tree, like the dead striped maple, change their sex as they age. Some species of mushroom have literally thousands of biological sexes!

Nature does not like binaries. When we look at all the weird and wonderful diversity in biological sex in other species, it puts the differences in sex and gender identity in our own species into perspective.

As a queer person with hormonal differences that, according to some doctors and activists, should be classified as an intersex condition, I find it deeply comforting to know that I'm in good company, with lots of binary-defying siblings throughout the kingdoms of animal, plant, and fungus.

Same-sex attraction is also very common in nature. In his book *Queer Ducks (and Other Animals): The Natural World of Animal Sexuality*, queer author Eliot Schrefer says that there is substantiated evidence of same-sex behavior in over 1,500 animal species.

Schrefer writes:

> The reasons for this recent bloom in reporting are twofold: research attention is finally being paid to the issue, and old taboos against publishing such results are eroding. In the past, scientists would avoid publishing on queer animal behavior because they found it shameful, or because they worried the establishment might then question the accuracy of their results... As recently as 1980, a US government document removed all references to homosexual behavior from a scientist's report on killer whales.

For centuries, scientists in the Western world have projected human ideas of gender and sexuality onto non-human animals. Data was misrepresented to maintain the belief that homosexuality in animals is rare. As scientists have begun to question these biases, the truth is becoming clear: same-sex relationships are a normal and healthy part of nature.

This homosexual behavior isn't limited to sexual activity. Some animals mate for life with members of the same sex, and bonded homosexual pairs have been observed raising offspring together, sometimes taking them in because the biological parents are unable to raise them. These pairs typically behave in more or less the same way as heterosexual pairs, and some of them have been observed turning down opposite-sex partners to stay with their chosen mates.

Animals have also been observed engaging in what we might call bisexual behavior. Some animals seem attracted to both male and female members of their species. In fact, bisexual animals may even have an evolutionary advantage!

In *Queer Ducks*, Schrefer discusses a theory called the "bisexual advantage," which states that fluid sexuality maximizes the chances for reproduction across a population.

Arguments that queerness is unnatural are disconnected from the reality of nature. If queerness were unhealthy or unnatural, it would not be so common in healthy non-human beings. To paraphrase a popular Internet meme, homosexuality is found in thousands of species, but homophobia is only found in one.

For queer people who have been hurt by claims that queerness goes against nature, it can be deeply healing to root ourselves in the messy, complex, and very queer web of life. Who we are is not only natural – it is a treasure that connects us with thousands of other beings throughout the web, from sex-changing trees and binary-defying mushrooms to gay penguins and bisexual bonobos.

If nature is sacred, then our queerness, being natural, must also be sacred.

Choosing a Queer Plant or Animal Ally

This activity will help you choose a plant or animal to connect with in your magical practice. Today we will be focused on allies who can help you embrace your queerness as something natural and beautiful, but you can also use this process when you want help in another area.

Start by doing some research online, or by reading a book about queer biology. Look for a plant or animal that reflects your own identity in some way. For example, as someone attracted to multiple genders, I might choose an animal known for high rates of bisexuality like dolphins, goats, or bonobos. If I was looking for an animal or plant ally for my sister, who is a binary transgender woman, I might choose a species known for changing its sex like maple trees, clownfish, or European common frogs.

Once you have chosen your ally, find an image of them that resonates with you. Spend a few minutes studying this image. What details do you notice? If you want, you can write down your observations.

Now, meditate on your chosen plant or animal. Try to do this in a place where you won't be disturbed for a few moments. You can use any meditation aids you want, such as music, incense, or noise-canceling headphones.

To meditate on your new ally, hold their image in your mind's eye. Think about your observations from earlier. Think about how they connect to your queer identity. Think about how both your identity and this plant/animal are natural and beautiful parts of the world.

Imagine your ally bringing you a message. This may not come in the form of words, especially if the ally you chose is a plant or a very non-human animal. Instead, you might experience a sudden rush of feelings, colors, or even smells and sounds. Pay attention to these messages, even if they don't make sense right away.

When you end your meditation, write down the message you received. If the message doesn't make sense right now, don't worry. Sometimes, we receive clarity after a few hours or days. You might even want to do some divination with a tool like tarot cards or a pendulum to ask for clarification.

Finally, ask yourself if you still feel like this plant or animal is the right spiritual ally for you at this time. Maybe you originally felt drawn to a certain species, but you didn't experience much of a connection during your meditation. If you feel like this species is not the right ally for you right now, simply repeat this exercise with a different plant or animal.

Once you have chosen an ally and made contact with them, you can call on their spirit in your practice. Lean on them when you need strength or guidance. Bring them into your spells. Ask them to help you overcome challenges, especially those related to your identity.

If you are asking a spirit for a favor, remember to repay them for their help. Offer clean water and compost to plant spirits. Offer animals some kind of food they might enjoy – for example, I might give fish or dry cat food to a cat spirit as a sign of my gratitude.

Chapter 6

Honoring Queer Ancestors

In 250 BCE, a young man living in the Roman Republic chose to dedicate his life to the goddess Cybele. As a *gallus*, a priest of the goddess, he would be castrated. Afterwards, he would dress in women's clothing, wear jewelry and makeup, and act in ways traditionally seen as feminine in Roman society. As part of a goddess cult that predated Rome, this gender-defying priest was an important part of his religious community.

In 100 AD, two men in Han China made love. As professional scholars, they were part of a culture in which love affairs between men were commonplace and were generally accepted. One or both of these lovers might marry a woman later, but this would not be seen as invalidating their earlier same-sex loves.

In 1040 AD, two young women living in an Italian convent fell in love. Though they lived in a Catholic society that condemned same-sex relationships, the privacy of the nunnery protected them from judgment.

These are only a few of the unnamed ancestors of modern queer communities. The names of many of our ancestors have been lost to time, but we can find signs of them in art, literature, and archaeological finds. Some of them lived in cultures that were accepting of their identities, and some of them didn't. All of them lived and loved in ways that might feel very familiar to modern queer folks.

There are also queer ancestors whose names and stories have survived through the centuries. These ancestors include:

- Sappho of Lesbos, the Ancient Greek poet who was known for her attraction to both men and women and whose legacy gave us the modern term, "lesbian".

- King Nzingha Mbande, the ruler of Ndongo and Matamba who was born a woman but demanded to be called king and who led their people in resistance against Portuguese invaders.
- The Public Universal Friend, a Quaker preacher who had a near death experience and was, by their own account, reborn without gender.
- Nikola Tesla, the inventor of the alternating current (AC) induction motor who openly expressed his lack of desire for sex.
- And many, many more.

For queer witches, these queer ancestors can be a family of powerful spiritual allies. Our ancestors were regular people, just like us. Of all the spirits we might work with, the ancestors are the ones who most understand and relate to our experiences and our struggles. They are able to share both our joys and our pains and can lend us some of their strength when we are struggling.

In my experience, ancestors are some of the easiest spirit guides to connect with. After all, we already have a connection with them through our shared identity and experiences. Even if we are not related to them by blood, we are part of a community they helped build. Like any good family, our ancestors care about us and want good things for us. They are often willing to step in and provide some spiritual aid to help us get those good things.

Ancestor veneration is one of the oldest forms of human spirituality, and honoring the ancestors in some way is common throughout the world, even today.

In East Asia, ancestor veneration is still an everyday part of many people's lives. In China, Japan, and other East Asian cultures, it is common for people to have ancestor shrines in their home. My favorites are the beautifully carved and lacquered shrine cabinets filled with photos of grandparents, great-grandparents, and other deceased loved ones. Maintaining this space is a sign of respect for those who have come before. Living descendants may make offerings of incense or fresh fruit to their honored dead.

The ancestors also play a big role in many West African cultures. Family is sacred in Yoruba culture and other related cultures. A person's children are said to be their wealth, while elders and ancestors are the keepers of wisdom, skills, and traditional knowledge.

This love and respect for the ancestors remains a big part of African Traditional Religions (ATRs), both in Africa and in the Americas. The ancestors are called the *egun* in Ifa (the indigenous religion of the Yoruba people). In Haitian Vodou, they are associated with the *gede,* the spirits who oversee the powers of death. In Hoodoo and other forms of African American folk magic, the ancestors are given a place of respect and honor in the home and may be called on for help alongside Christian saints and angels.

In North Africa, ancestor veneration dates back at least to Kemet, the civilization we now call ancient Egypt. Archaeologists have found the remains of ancestor shrines in Kemetic homes. These shrines included statuettes or busts of deceased family members, who were honored with offerings by their living descendants. There is also some evidence that the people of Kemet visited the tombs of their ancestors to leave offerings of food and drink.

Europe's history of ancestor veneration stretches back at least to ancient Rome, where most households kept a *lararium,* a shrine to the *lares*. The lares are guardians of the family and the household, and this group of spirits included human ancestors. A Roman lararium might contain images of the lares of that family, including images of the honored dead. Offerings were made at these household shrines, and the lares and *parentes* (immediate family members who had died) were honored each year at the *Parentalia*, a nine-day festival in February.

Other European cultures had a similar respect for their ancestors. For example, in Old Norse culture, the *dísir* were feminine protective spirits, believed to be feminine ancestors. This group of spirits was honored with sacrifices at the *Dísablót* festival each year.

Even after Europe's conversion to Christianity, veneration for the honored dead remained in the form of the saints. In Catholic theology, saints are dead humans who have entered Heaven and who can be called on to help the living. The most famous saints are probably Saint Mary and Saint Joseph, the mother and foster father of Jesus. Most Catholic churches contain a shrine to the Holy Family off to one side of the sanctuary, where churchgoers can honor Mary, Joseph, and Jesus. Some churches may also have shrines to other saints, such as Saint Jude or Saint Francis of Assisi. It is not uncommon for Catholics to choose a personal patron saint, who they work with closely and have a special relationship with.

The ancestors also have a place of honor in many indigenous North American cultures. Iroquois cultures see the ancestors as everyday guardians who can choose to communicate with their descendants to share wisdom and offer guidance. Some Blackfoot people carried their ancestors' skeletons in rawhide bags as a sign of devotion and respect. Like the Romans and Egyptians, Anasazi people honored their ancestors with shrines that included images of the beloved dead.

The Mexica people, sometimes called the Aztecs, honored the dead with a huge festival each year. In modern Mexico, these ancient beliefs have mixed with the Catholic Feast of All Souls to become *el Dia de los Muertos* ("the Day of the Dead"). During this festival, people have picnics at their loved ones' graves and build beautiful colored shrines called *ofrendas*. It is a joyful celebration that honors the lives of those who have passed on.

In the past, modern witchcraft and paganism has been more focused on deities than on human ancestors, but there has been a push in recent years to restore the beloved dead to their rightful place as honored spiritual guides. It is now common, for example, for witches who follow the Wheel of the Year to honor their ancestors when celebrating the feast of Samhain each autumn. Some groups include a moment honoring the beloved dead in every ritual. There is even growing interest in reviving the ancestor veneration of past cultures – after all, what better way to honor your ancestors than by relearning their own cultural practices?

All of this is wonderful, but ancestor work can be tricky for those of us with strained relationships with our living families. How can we draw power from our family line if our living family has rejected us because of our identity? How can we honor our ancestors when they were part of a cycle of abuse that has victimized us? How can we reconcile love for our ancestors with generational trauma?

This is where our chosen family comes in. No one is under any obligation to have a relationship with the family that raised them – and that goes for both living and dead family members. If you truly feel that you cannot have a healthy relationship with someone, you should do what is best for you and your wellbeing, no matter which side of the veil that person is on.

Chosen family is an important part of the queer community. In the past, queer people who were disowned by their families or who had to cut ties for their own health and safety went on to form their own family groups with other queer people.

Sometimes these chosen families had a formal structure, like the houses of 19th and 20th century *ballroom subculture*. Also known as ball culture or the ballroom scene, this colorful subculture was created by Black and Latine queer folks as a response to racism in drag. In the ballroom scene, *houses* are chosen families that support each other within the culture.

Many iconic aspects of today's queer culture, like voguing and many slang terms, come from ball culture.

In other cases, a chosen family was simply a group of queer people who chose to live together and support each other. Even today, when queer people are less likely to be automatically disowned for coming out, chosen family remains an important part of the community.

Your real family, the ones who really matter, are the people you choose and who choose you back. They are the people who share your joys and your sorrows, the people you can count on to be there for you in a crisis. For some of us, that includes the people who raised us. For others, it doesn't, and that's okay.

Chosen families are the living family we choose. Chosen ancestors are the ancestral spirits we choose to honor in our practice. Like with a chosen family, our chosen ancestors may include some people we are actually related to and others we have no legal or biological link with but still feel a strong connection to. Some witches may choose not to work with any of their legal or biological ancestors, and that doesn't make their practice any less valid.

Your chosen ancestors will include any members of your chosen family who have died. Maybe this includes your grandmother, who set aside her conservative political beliefs to support you when you came out. Maybe it includes the older gay man who took you under his wing when you were new to the community and still figuring things out. Maybe it includes your childhood best friend's mom who was always willing to make space for you in her home. Anyone you consider family or a close friend who has died would be a wonderful addition to your ancestor work practice.

You might also choose to honor ancestors you never met, but who still helped you, comforted you, or inspired you in some way. These are the spirits author Patti Wigington calls *spiritual kinfolk* in her book, *Badass Ancestors: Finding Your Power with Ancestral Guides*.

In her book, Wigington says that:

> Our spiritual kinfolk are the ones who have directly shaped our thoughts, beliefs, and ideas to help frame the person we have become.

This includes the authors whose books defined your childhood, the founders of the religious or spiritual tradition(s) you belong to, and the historical figures you wanted to be just like when you grew up, along with anyone else who has helped shape the person you are today.

For queer witches, our spiritual kinfolk includes the people who fought for our rights, who inspired us to come out of the closet, or whose stories made us feel less alone. The queer ancestors we discussed earlier in this chapter are all our spiritual kinfolk, because without them, we would not be here and be queer in the way we are today.

I keep a shrine to my queer ancestors in my home, next to some photos and mementos of my deceased family members. This shrine includes images of Achilles and Sappho, who represent all past men who loved men and all past women who loved women, respectively. It also includes images of Freddie Mercury and Marsha P. Johnson, two more recent queer ancestors that I feel a special admiration for. It could just as easily include images of Oscar Wilde, Stormé DeLarverie, Sylvia Rivera, Gilbert Baker, Frida Kahlo, or countless other queer icons whose lives inspire me every day.

As far as I know, none of these people are related to me, but they've had a greater impact on my life than any of my biological ancestors further back than my great-grandparents. Why wouldn't I celebrate them in my practice?

If you have chosen ancestors you'd like to bring into your magical practice, the best way to start is by creating a shrine for them.

Creating a Queer Ancestor Shrine

A *shrine* is a special place that serves as a home (or at least a visiting space) for one or more spirits. Because of this, you should approach shrine-building with the same care you would use to prepare a space for an honored guest in your home.

This is especially true when choosing the location for your shrine. It's best to keep shrines out of the bathroom. You wouldn't expect a houseguest to sleep by the toilet, and it would be rude to stick your ancestors there.

Other inappropriate locations for your ancestor shrine include garages, storage sheds, and supply closets. You want to avoid putting a shrine in a space that doesn't get used often, because out-of-the-way shrines are easy to forget about and may become neglected.

You'll also want to think twice before putting your ancestor shrine in your bedroom. If you use your bedroom exclusively for sleep and relaxation, it's probably fine to place your ancestors there. But if your bedroom is your go-to space for sex and physical intimacy, you probably don't want to put Grandma in there. If it would be awkward to share that space with a living family member, don't put your ancestor shrine there.

As for the space itself, shrines can be built on any flat surface. I find desktops and coffee tables make for excellent shrines, but I have also used the top shelf of a bookshelf and a designated space on my kitchen counter. You can even purchase special cabinets designed especially for use as shrines.

It's best for shrines to be permanent whenever possible. Constantly building, taking down, and rebuilding a shrine makes it harder to develop stable, permanent relationships with the spirits that shrine is dedicated to.

If you're limited on space, try to build a small, permanent shrine instead of a larger, temporary one. Your ancestor shrine could be a corner of your desk or a windowsill. If you move around frequently, try building a portable shrine inside a shoe box or jewelry box.

Once you've chosen a space, think about the ancestors you plan to include in your shrine. Will you be including ancestors from your family of origin, or will you be working exclusively with your spiritual kin? Are there any specific people you want to honor?

Depending on which ancestors you want to include, it may be a good idea to separate them into more than one shrine. An ancestor shrine is sort of like a family reunion – and just like at family reunions, strong personalities can clash and cause conflict. If two of your ancestors had a lifelong feud or fought and died on opposite sides of a war, you probably wouldn't want to put them next to each other in your shrine.

The easiest way to separate groups of ancestors who might otherwise butt heads is to divide your shrine into sections. For example, maybe you divide your shrine space down the middle and put one group of ancestors on the left and the other group on the right. This can also be a good way to honor ancestors from different cultures, and can lead to some very striking decoration choices.

If you're setting up your shrine on a flat surface, choose an altar cloth as a base. A plain white cloth is a good all-purpose option. Any cloth will work as long as it is clean and in good condition. (No stains or holes, please!) You probably already have a sheet, dish towel, or scarf that will make a fine altar cloth.

You can also choose a cloth in a color or pattern that you associate with your ancestors, like red silk to honor Chinese ancestors or a lace mantilla to honor Mexican Catholic ancestors. For a shrine dedicated to queer ancestors, you could even use a Pride flag as your altar cloth. I am especially fond of the original Pride flag designed by Gilbert Baker, which features the rainbow colors of the modern flag as well as a hot pink stripe representing sex and a turquoise stripe representing magic.

Once you've spread out your altar cloth, start filling the space with images of ancestors you want to honor. This could include photos of your deceased loved ones, paintings, or even statuettes of historical figures. Make sure you only include images of people who have already died, because it's considered bad luck to put an image of a living person on a shrine dedicated to the dead.

You can also include items that are linked to your ancestors. If you have items that actually belonged to your ancestors, these are a wonderful addition to your shrine. For example, my ancestor shrine includes some of my grandfather's books.

You can also use art created by your ancestors. In a shrine dedicated to queer ancestors, you might include a copy of one of Virginia Woolf's or Oscar Wilde's books, for example.

You might also include items that symbolically represent your ancestors. My queer ancestor shrine includes a pink triangle pin (a symbol of queer oppression used by Nazis, later reclaimed as a symbol of queer strength), an image of a labrys (a symbol used by lesbians in the 20th century), and a charm I created to represent my wishes for the future of the LGBTQ+ community.

The final and most important part of your shrine is an offering vessel. This is a bowl, cup, or other dish where you can leave offerings for your ancestors. It's best practice to have two vessels, one for liquids and one for solids.

There are several optional finishing touches you can include, depending on your space. Candles, incense burners, and vases full of flowers are all traditional inclusions in an ancestor shrine, but none of them are required.

Accessibility Adjustment: If you are unable to create a permanent shrine, even a portable one, try finding an alternative way to honor your ancestors. Your "shrine" could be a photo album filled with images of your ancestors, or a box of trinkets that remind you of them. You can also create virtual shrines with websites like WordPress, Tumblr, and Pinterest. (A virtual shrine is typically a collection of images that invoke a spirit or group of spirits.)

Working with the Ancestors

Once you have a shrine, you'll want to begin making regular offerings to your ancestors. Offerings are the foundation of any working relationship with a spirit or group of spirits. Frequent offerings establish a relationship based on *reciprocity* (mutual giving). In reciprocal relationships, both people involved care for each other, and both people benefit from the relationship. We don't just make offerings to our ancestors because we want something from them, but as a way of showing our love and respect for them.

When we honor our ancestors, we are caring for them and keeping their memories alive. Cultures as ancient and widespread as ancient Kemet (Egypt), China, and pre-Christian Scandinavia all shared a belief that the comfort, wellbeing, or even safety of souls in the afterlife depended on support from their living descendants. By making offerings, we "feed" the ancestors' spirits and keep their memories alive.

In turn, our ancestors care for us in the way only they can, by intervening on our behalf in spiritual matters. Just as we make offerings out of love for them, they provide spiritual help because they love us and want us to do well. This cycle of gift-giving from a place of mutual care is the core of spirit work in queer witchcraft.

Fresh water is used as an offering to the ancestors in many different cultures. I recommend keeping a glass of fresh water in your ancestor shrine at all times, as a way of keeping the space welcoming to your kin. Just make sure you change out the water once a day and switch out the glass once a week to avoid mold and other issues.

Other common offerings that seem to be well-received by just about all ancestors include coffee, tea, liquor, and fresh flowers. Any of these would be an appropriate offering for your ancestors, with the exception of liquor if the ancestor you're working with didn't drink in life or was in recovery from an alcohol addiction. Freshly brewed coffee seems to be a favorite for my ancestors and is one of my go-to offerings for them.

You can also offer your ancestors things they enjoyed while they were alive. I have never used tobacco recreationally, but I burn it as an offering to my grandfather, who smoked and chewed throughout his life. I often offer candy because my ancestors tended to have big sweet tooths. Giving your ancestors the things they love is a sure way to get in their good graces.

How often you make offerings is up to you. Once a week is a good start, but if you're especially busy you might start with monthly offerings. Some witches make offerings every day, and others only make offerings when they feel like their ancestors are asking for something. What you do is between you and your ancestors.

Problem Ancestors

Our ancestors were human beings, and like all human beings, they had flaws. Some of them did great things, and some of them did terrible things. Some of them were humanitarian superheroes, and some of them were total scum. None of them were perfect. All of them had people who loved them, and most of them probably believed that what they were doing was justified, no matter what we may think today.

While I do believe that we choose our family, both living and dead, I also want to be very clear that this is not a free pass to avoid all work with challenging ancestors. You may be tempted to reject any ancestors who did bad things or who had beliefs we now view as problematic, but this stunts our practice and can trap us in a feedback loop of wishful thinking.

Because of the sheer number of people we are related to, I can guarantee every one of us is descended from at least one murderer, rapist, slaveholder, or other human monster. That legacy is part of our inheritance, for better or worse, and reckoning with the pain and ugliness our ancestors were responsible for is an important part of this work.

I have ancestors who owned slaves and ancestors who were enslaved. I have ancestors who fled famines, wars, and oppression in Europe only to become complicit in white supremacy in the United States. I have ancestors who were English nobility and ancestors who were Scottish freedom fighters. I have ancestors who were Confederate soldiers and ancestors who worked as abolitionists in the years leading up to the Civil War. I have one ancestor who was Cherokee and who secured his family's right to remain in the Southeastern US by volunteering to work as a translator for the US government on the Trail of Tears, actively helping force other Cherokee people to leave their homes forever. All of them are a part of my family's history, and I am living in the world they helped create, whether I like it or not.

I will never invite my ancestors who owned slaves into my sacred space, but I will also not deny what they did. Instead, I accept the lesson that none of us comes from a "pure" ancestry and work hard to right the wrongs of my ancestors. I genuinely believe that facing those wrongs with honesty and humility is some of the most important spiritual work I will do in this lifetime.

The same goes for spiritual or community ancestors. Every community has its bad parts, and the queer community is no exception. Some of the most vocal champions of queer liberation have been violently racist, misogynistic, antisemitic, or otherwise bigoted. History is full of queer warmongers and war criminals. To deny this part of our community's history would be just as harmful as denying the problematic ancestors in our family trees.

An example of one of these difficult ancestors in the queer community is Aleister Crowley. Crowley was fairly open about his bisexuality, and he is also one of the most influential ancestors of modern Western occultism, including modern witchcraft. And, in many ways, he was problematic. He was very much a racist, a misogynist, and an antisemite. He established many issues around race, gender, and sex in occultism that we are still wrestling with today. And yet, he is still a part of our history both as witches and as queer people.

Am I going to give Crowley a place of honor in my ancestor shrine? No. But I think it would do more harm than good if I pretended he never existed or erased the history of his contributions to modern occultism. As someone who regularly uses ritual elements influenced by Crowley (like nearly all modern witches do), I have a responsibility to be honest about this history. I also have a responsibility to work on doing better in my own practice.

We can't change history, but we can learn from it. All we can do is take the legacy we've been handed and do our best to leave a better world for future generations.

Chapter 7

Queering Divinity

For many queer people, the word "God" is uncomfortable. It is a word that has been used to exclude, persecute, and even harm us. For many queer people, especially in the United States and Western Europe, God is judgment. God is punishment. God is a threat to our very lives as queer people.

At the time of this book's writing, the Christian God is being used by right-wing politicians in the United States to justify an unprecedented wave of anti-LGBTQ+ and especially anti-transgender laws.

And yet, many queer people are deeply spiritual. There is a growing understanding in our communities that our collective healing and liberation must include spiritual connection. We deserve not only safety and protection for our rights, but healing for our souls as well.

A growing number of young queer people are seeking that soul healing in paganism and witchcraft. In a 2022 article for NBC, Antonio Pagliarulo described witchcraft – which they define as including "Wicca, paganism, folk magic and other New Age traditions" – as one of the fastest growing spiritual paths in America. This boom in popularity has roots in the Second Wave Feminism of the 1960s and 1970s, when many feminists took up Goddess worship as an alternative to patriarchal religions. Witchcraft offers us the chance to connect with the divine in ways that do not reinforce a culture of misogyny, homophobia, and transphobia.

However, many of the queer witches and pagans I have spoken to do not see their own identities reflected in magical spaces.

Several of the queer folks I spoke to while working on this book expressed discomfort with rituals that focus on images and descriptions of heterosexual sex, pregnancy, and birth. Several people also said they were uncomfortable with the emphasis on masculine vs. feminine energy in modern witchcraft. While these approaches work well for some witches, it is clear that we need more inclusive models if we want everyone to feel welcome in our ritual circle.

As queer people, we deserve to see ourselves reflected in the gods we worship. We deserve rituals that are inclusive of our experiences. We deserve to form meaningful relationships with the divine, whatever that looks like for us as individuals.

Not every witch will feel called to include deities in their practice, and that's okay. I have saved this topic for later in the book because I know it can be deeply uncomfortable for many queer folks to even consider things like worship and prayer. Religious trauma is real, and it is normal to feel uncomfortable, anxious, or triggered as a result.

For some people, the best way to heal is to reject deity work entirely and focus their practice solely on magic, or on other spirits like ancestors and nature spirits. That is an entirely valid way to practice witchcraft, and if that is what works best for you I encourage you to pursue it. Feel free to skip this chapter and the next.

On the other hand, some queer people want to have a relationship with deity, but they feel excluded from worship because of their identity. For these people, I want to provide some suggestions for queering our relationship with deity and some examples of queer gods, goddesses, and holy ones from pantheons around the world.

It is important to keep these myths and stories alive, as a reminder that queer people have always existed and have always been holy.

How Myth Shapes Reality

In many ways, our understanding of the gods and what they represent shapes our understanding of the world around us. For example, modern Western culture's issues around sex, gender, and sexuality can be directly traced back to the dominant religious narratives in our culture.

To avoid speaking negatively of other people's faiths, I want to share an example from my own life. I grew up in a politically conservative offshoot of Christianity. This group had many of the traits of a cult, as defined by Stevan Hassan's BITE model, a tool used to identify methods of control used by cult groups. The group was (and still is) known for homophobia, as well as racism and misogyny. While, of course, most Christians do not share these bigoted beliefs, they were the norm in the church I was raised in.

As a child, I was taught religious stories that reinforced this bigoted worldview. For example, I was told that the universe was created single-handedly by a male/masculine God. After creating the world, God created the first man. When God saw that the man was lonely, He took one of the man's ribs and used it to create the first woman. God gave the first humans one command: be fruitful and multiply, i.e., have sex and make lots of babies. God also created a test for them: do not pursue forbidden knowledge, and you will live forever. Of course, the Devil tempted the woman to break this commandment, and God punished the human race with suffering and death because of her sin.

This creation story enforces certain views of sex, gender, and sexuality. First, it implies that because God is male/masculine, men are closer to the divine than women. Second, it implies that women were created to serve men, or at least to fulfill men's needs. Third, it implies that heterosexual sex, specifically for the purpose of reproduction, is the correct, or at least most holy, expression of human sexuality. And finally, it implies that women are more weak-willed and sinful than men.

With myths like this, it is no wonder my childhood religious community was so full of misogyny and homophobia. Only men were allowed to preach or perform sacraments. Women were allowed to hold support roles only, and were always subservient to male leadership. Girls were told from a young age that the most holy thing they could do was get married and have children, but boys were never given the same talk. Members of the church who felt same-sex attraction or gender dysphoria were encouraged to "pray the gay away," sometimes with the help of conversion therapy. If someone chose to live openly as a queer person, they were ostracized from the church community.

I want to make a note that, while the faith I was raised in was Christian, myths that reinforce social bias are not just a Christian problem. Any group of any faith can fall into this trap, especially if the group's leadership is openly involved in anti-LGBTQ+ politics. Group leaders may twist religious stories to better fit their own beliefs.

How would our spiritual communities look different if we had different myths? What would it look like if we had sacred stories that uplifted differences in sex and gender instead of enforcing a hierarchy? What would it look like if we worshiped gods who were explicitly described in the myths as queer? These are the questions queer people across many different religions are beginning to ask.

An important part of my personal recovery from religious trauma was learning about different creation myths. I wanted to look at how different cultures remembered the creation of their world, and to look at how those myths enforced cultural biases. I wanted to look at who was included in creation narratives and who wasn't, and I hoped to find some stories about people who were like me.

I found that the myth of a single, male/masculine creator God is far from universal.

In Shinto, the traditional religion of Japan, the goddess Izanami and the god Izanagi are said to have created the islands of Japan together. Iroquois peoples in North America tell the story of Sky Woman, a goddess figure who fell from the Skyworld and, with the help of the animals, danced the world into being. In Yoruba mythology from West Africa, the orisha tasked with creating humans was Obatala, who author and spiritual leader Luisah Teish says is "always both male and female" in her book *Jambalaya: The Natural Woman's Book of Personal Charms and Practical Rituals*. I encourage readers to seek out stories of these creator deities told by members of their own cultures and religions.

As I researched the creation myths of Europe, North Africa, and West Asia, I discovered a common theme. Many different cultures, across time and space, told stories of an intersex/androgynous creator deity who was the ancestor of all the other gods. This motif appeared again and again, and each time I came across a different version of this concept I felt moved in a way I never had by the patriarchal creation myth I grew up with. Here was a Creator who was both man and woman, and both, and neither.

Below, I present three different creation stories featuring this motif of an androgynous/intersex Creator, from three different cultures separated by thousands of years. This is not to argue that these are all different versions of one true creation story. Instead, I want to show how this idea has manifested differently in different cultures. As you read these stories, consider what implications they have for human sex, gender, and sexuality.

Our first creation myth comes from Ancient Kemet, called Egypt by modern scholars. This civilization lasted for thousands of years, through shifting dynastic politics, and many different creation myths rose and fell in popularity over time.

One of the older and more popular Kemetic creation myths, which was recorded in Yunu (called Heliopolis by the Greeks) during the Old Kingdom, features the sun god Atum-Ra as the androgynous creator of the world. The version given here is adapted from the book *Temple of the Cosmos* by Jeremy Naydler.

In the beginning, there was only the dark, infinite waters of Nun. Within Nun, everything was formless and nothing was separate from anything else. But within the waters of Nun, a spark of life began to stir.

This spark of life was the creative principle, which is called Atum. The name Atum means "to be complete." For an immeasurable time before time, Atum rested in the waters, alone and inert.

Eventually, something changed. Atum began to recognize themself as an individual, separate from the waters surrounding them.

This act of self-recognition was the first act of creation, and it was in this moment that the world was born. For Atum is the god of being, and so everything that exists is Atum.

At that moment, Atum took on the form of the sacred scarab beetle, KhepRer, whose name means "the becoming one." Atum-as-KhepRer emerged from the waters of Nun and the First Land burst forth out of the waters.

On the First Land, a reed took root and grew into the World Tree. When the World Tree was grown, a brilliant, shining bird flew out of the darkness and landed in the Tree's branches. This bird was Ra, the sun. And Ra is also Atum.

For as long as the Kemetic religion was practiced, Atum, Ra, and KhepRer were all understood as different aspects of one being.

Atum was alone on the First Land, and as the creative principle, they longed to create new beings. Atum, who is called "the Great He-She," became aroused and began to masturbate. (Ancient texts explicitly describe this as Atum taking their penis in their hand.)

When Atum reached orgasm, the first gods, Shu and Tefnut were born from their climax. Shu is the god of air and space, and Tefnut is the goddess of moisture. Shu and Tefnut are the parents of Geb, the god of the earth, and Nut, the goddess of the sky, and Geb and Nut are the parents of all other things.

One of the most interesting things about this myth is that Atum, the first being, was able to reproduce without a partner because they contained within themself both the male and the female principles.

The Great He-She is the supreme deity, and Atum-Ra was the center of the pantheon in Yunu. Atum-Ra's androgynous nature is not judged, but celebrated. As their name implies, Atum is complete in a way that the other gods, who require partners to create life, are not.

The sun and the waters (represented by the annual flooding of the Nile river) were the two most important elements of life in Kemetic culture, which depended on farming. Because of the fertile soil and regular flooding that allowed crops to flourish, this Kemetic creation story depicts the creation of the world as an act of loving creative expression by the sun god.

Other cultures in other places had a more challenging relationship with their environment, and as a result their stories depict creation as a struggle. The Norse people were the ancestors of modern Scandinavian cultures. They were one of the last cultures in Europe to convert to Christianity and are probably best known for their *viking* (pronounced "VEE-king") raids on their Christian neighbors. Parts of the Norse world had a subarctic climate, with long, harsh winters and short, cool summers. For example, in modern Iceland, there are as few as four hours of sunlight per day during the winter.

One version of the Norse creation myth was recorded around 1220 CE by an Icelandic monk named Snorri Sturluson, long after the conversion of Iceland to Christianity. Although fragments of older versions of the myth have survived, Snorri's version is one of the most complete accounts. The version of the Norse creation myth given here is adapted from Snorri's *Prose Edda*.

In the beginning, there were two primordial realms: Muspelheim, the realm of light and fire, which was so hot life could not survive it, and Niflheim, the realm of ice and frost, which was so cold life could not survive it. Between Muspelheim and Niflheim was Ginnungagap, the great void.

Over uncountable years, the cold, wet air of Niflheim and the warm light of Muspelheim met in Ginnungagap and mixed. From this mingling of fire and ice, the first being was created. This was Ymir, the first *jotun* (a type of primordial god or nature spirit). Ymir was the parent of the first jotuns. A man and a woman grew under one of their arms, and one of their legs begot a son with the other.

Another being was born from the frost, like Ymir – this was Audhumla, the primordial cow whose milk fed Ymir. Audhumla licked the rime of the ice until she eventually uncovered a beautiful, shining man named Buri. Buri had a son named Bor, and Bor married one of Ymir's daughters and had three sons: Odin, Vili, and Vé.

These three brothers took it upon themselves to kill Ymir so that a world could be made from their giant body. After slaying the first being, the brothers took their body to Ginnungagap and began to fill the empty space.

No part of the body was wasted. From Ymir's blood came the seas and lakes. From their flesh came the earth. From their hair came the trees, and from their bones came the mountains. Even Ymir's teeth were used to make rocks. Ymir's skull became the sky, and their brains became the clouds. And thus Odin, Vili, and Vé made the world from the body of Ymir.

Heathen author Ryan Smith suggests that the Norse creation myth can be interpreted as a revolution overthrowing an unjust power.

In his book, *The Way of Fire and Ice: The Living Tradition of Norse Paganism,* Smith writes:

> Under Ymir, only the great giant feasted on the only source of wealth in all existence. The hoarding and poverty of their lives led Odin, Vili, and Ve to rebellion. In cooperation with the rest of the gods, they then used Ymir's body to fashion a new world where all would have space to thrive.

This Norse myth is very different from the Kemetic creation myth we discussed earlier, but there are some notable similarities. Like Atum, Ymir is an androgynous/intersex being with the ability to reproduce without a partner. Both Atum and Ymir are the parent or grandparent of all the other gods in their pantheons. However, Ymir is not the one who creates the world – instead, Ymir must be defeated so their descendants can create a habitable world. What cultural differences might be reflected in these different myths?

The final creation myth I want to share here is much more recent, and is a product of modern witchcraft. The story of the Star Goddess was first recorded by Victor Anderson, one of the founders of the Feri tradition of witchcraft. Star Goddess is still an important part of Feri, as well as the Reclaiming tradition, which is influenced by Feri. Star Goddess has even been adopted by some Wiccans and solitary witches.

As a truly modern example of the androgynous/intersex creator deity, Star Goddess reflects the values and beliefs of modern witches. While newer, the story is just as powerful as myths from long-dead cultures.

One of the most well-known versions of the story of Star Goddess is recorded by Starhawk, one of the founders of Reclaiming, in her book *The Spiral Dance: A Rebirth of the Ancient Religion of the Great Goddess*. I find Starhawk's version of this myth especially beautiful, so I have chosen to quote it here in full instead of paraphrasing:

> Alone, awesome, complete within Herself, the Goddess, She whose name cannot be spoken, floated in the abyss of the outer darkness, before the beginning of all things. And as She looked into the curved mirror of black space, She saw by her own light her radiant reflection, and fell in love with it. She drew it forth by the power that was in Her and made love to Herself, and called Her 'Miria, the Wonderful.'
>
> Their ecstasy burst forth in the single song of all that is, was, or ever shall be, and with the song came motion, waves that poured outward and became all the spheres and circles of the worlds. The Goddess became filled with love, swollen with love, and She gave birth to a rain of bright spirits that filled the worlds and became all beings.
>
> But in that great movement, Miria was swept away, and as She moved out from the Goddess She became more masculine. First She became the Blue God, the gentle, laughing God of love. Then She became the Green One, vine-covered, rooted in the earth, the spirit of all growing things. At last She became the Horned God, the Hunter whose face is the ruddy sun and yet dark as Death. But always desire draws Him back toward the Goddess, so that He circles her eternally, seeking to return in love.
>
> All began in love; all seeks to return to love. Love is the law, the teacher of wisdom, and the great revealer of mysteries.

The influence of modern occultism is very clear in this story, especially the last two sentences. The use of she/her pronouns to refer to the supreme being shows the influence of Second Wave Feminism. And yet, the Goddess has striking similarities to Atum and Ymir.

Like Atum, the Goddess is described as a complete being, and like in Atum's story, it is an act of masturbation that births the other gods. Like Ymir, the Goddess is able to impregnate Herself. She is the source of all things, and Her love is the spark that ignites the Big Bang.

While Starhawk uses she/her pronouns to describe the Goddess, she could just as easily be described with they/them pronouns, as I have chosen to describe Atum and Ymir. The Star Goddess is explicitly understood to transcend gender and to contain all possible genders and biological sexes within Herself.

Think for a moment about how our culture would change if one of these three myths was our dominant creation narrative. How would things be different if the entire world was understood to be the product of a perfectly androgynous God/dess? How might that change the way we think about sex, gender, and sexuality? Pondering these questions is part of how we do the work of queering divinity.

Chapter 8

The Queer Gods

While comparing different myths can be a useful mental exercise, the real work of queering the divine lies in building relationships with individual deities. Witchcraft is experiential, and reading about a god or goddess, while definitely important, cannot replace genuine connection.

Many witches choose to work with deities from historic pantheons. A witch might worship Hellenic (Greek), Kemetic (Egyptian), or Norse deities, for example. Another witch might work with sacred figures from other Western occult traditions like Thelema, ceremonial magic, or Goetia. Some witches work with the Goddess and God, the two-part divinity worshiped in Wicca.

In her book on animism, *The Wakeful World,* Emma Restall Orr describes the gods as "the most powerful spirits or patterns of nature's configurations of interaction."

Deities are forces of nature, human concepts, or ideals filtered through cultural knowledge. For example, Aphrodite, Hathor, and Freyja can all be called goddesses of love, but they are very different from each other. Their differences reflect how the concept of love was viewed differently in Hellenic, Kemetic, and Norse cultures.

To claim that Aphrodite and Freyja are the same or are interchangeable for one another would be just as ridiculous as claiming that Hellenic and Norse culture are the same or are interchangeable. It is disrespectful not only to these goddesses but to the cultures that originally worshiped them.

While deities are the personification (or soul, if you prefer) of cultural concepts, on some level they are also people like us.

Like us, deities have their own personalities, likes, dislikes, and agendas. Like us, they have free will.

It is important to remember that when we interact with a deity, we are interacting both with a human-like personality *and* with a force of nature. Building a working relationship with a deity requires at least a basic understanding of their original worship and culture. While it doesn't take an Egyptology degree to worship Isis, for example, it is helpful to know how religion worked in ancient Kemet and what Isis represented to ancient Kemetic people. It is also a sign of respect for the deity to take the time to get to know them.

It is beyond the scope of this book to give readers this level of knowledge for all of the historic deities mentioned. Instead, the goal of this chapter is to provide brief examples of gods, goddesses, and others who are associated with queer identity.

If one of the deities mentioned here catches your interest, I hope you will do your own research as you begin a relationship with them. See the "References" section at the end of this book for resources to help with your search.

I use "queer" in this book to refer to identities and experiences outside modern Western cultural norms, especially binary gender and straight romantic or sexual relationships. But we should remember that modern Western norms are not universal.

The deities presented here resonate with modern queer experiences, but they may not have been "queer" by the standards of their original culture. This is especially true in cultures that acknowledged three or more genders or that recognized multiple types of romantic and sexual relationships.

Our knowledge of historic queer deities is limited by two things: 1.) how accepting their culture was of identities we would now identify as queer, and 2.) how much documentation from that culture has survived.

For example, in ancient Hellenic culture, bisexuality was a cultural norm, especially for men. Hellenic cultures, especially Athens, also left behind a lot of writing and art that has survived to the modern day. Because of this, we know that nearly every masculine deity in the Hellenic pantheon was known to take male lovers, and that some goddesses were also described in same-sex relationships.

There are almost certainly queer deities and myths that have been lost to time, either because they were never written down or because those writings were destroyed. There are also probably gods we know today who were seen as queer by their original worshipers, but this aspect of their worship has been lost.

Reconstructing historic religion is an imperfect art, with many gaps in our knowledge of the past. The best we can do is honor the old ways by celebrating the parts of them that have survived.

Queer Gods of the Kemetic Pantheon

As we have already discussed, ancient Kemetic culture viewed the supreme creator as androgynous. One of Atum's titles is "The Great He-She," and they are both mother and father to the entire Kemetic pantheon. Other queer Kemetic deities include Set, Horus, Hapi, and possibly Nephthys.

Set and Horus are depicted as rivals in most modern versions of their myths. Set rules the deserts of Upper Egypt and is associated with storms and natural disasters. Horus rules the fertile lands of Lower Egypt and is associated with the sun and the pharaoh. Set is said to have killed Horus's father Osiris. When Horus became an adult, he defeated Set and took his rightful place as the king of the gods.

This rivalry has survived in modern pop culture, but originally there was also a homoerotic relationship between these gods. Ancient Kemetic texts depict Set and Horus as sexual partners.

In one myth, Set tries to humiliate Horus by exposing him as the receptive partner in their sex (the "bottom," to use modern slang), showing that Set had literally dominated him. Horus, with help from his mother Isis, turns the table on Set. When Set attempts to humiliate Horus, Set is revealed as the receptive partner instead.

This myth implies that Egypt, like many other cultures, may not have viewed homosexuality itself as shameful but had taboos against men taking on a receptive role in the bedroom.

It's worth noting that how healthy the relationship between these two male gods was varies from one account to another. Some sources describe Set as predatory, or even depict him sexually assaulting Horus. Other sources show Horus as a willing and enthusiastic participant. These different versions might reflect changing attitudes towards same-sex relationships over the thousands of years of Kemetic civilization.

Hapi, the god of the Nile river, is depicted as intersex in art and hieroglyphics. Hapi is typically shown with both a beard and breasts, and Kemetic sources refer to him with masculine pronouns. As the personification of the Nile's annual flood, Hapi is associated with fertility and new life.

Explicit depictions of queer women are harder to find in Kemetic mythology, but some scholars believe the goddess Nephthys was understood to be a lesbian by her worshipers. This interpretation is controversial, but scholars who defend this theory point to Nephthys's marriage to Set, a deity much more explicitly associated with homosexuality. Set and Nephthys have no children, although some sources say that Nephthys is the mother of Anubis, fathered by Osiris.

Nephthys and Set are rarely depicted together in art or myths. When Set killed Osiris, Nephthys sided with Osiris's widow Isis instead of with her own husband. Nephthys and Isis raised Horus together, and Nephthys supported Horus's claim to the throne.

Nephthys and Isis were frequently worshiped together, and they share many of the same associations. Like Isis, Nephthys is associated with childbirth, magic, and protection. Some scholars argue that Isis and Nephthys can be interpreted as lovers.

While Nephthys's status as a lesbian is debated in the academic world, what we can say for sure is that she is a divine role model for women and femme people who choose not to become wives or mothers, and for people who choose to leave an unhappy marriage. She, Isis, and Horus can also be invoked as gods of found and chosen family, which is an important part of queer communities.

Queer Gods of the Hellenic Pantheon

Hellenic religion was much more explicit about which of the gods were queer. As previously mentioned, most major Hellenic gods have at least one myth that describes them in a same-sex relationship. Hellenic deities with an especially strong connection to queer identity are Apollo, Dionysus, Artemis, and Aphrodite. Hellenic myths also include stories of explicitly transgender deities, such as Caeneus.

Both Apollo and Dionysus were associated with same-sex relationships between men, and the very different reputations of these gods show us that queerness was normal across all levels of Hellenic society.

Apollo was possibly the most beloved god in the Hellenic pantheon. Alongside Zeus and Hestia, he was one of the only gods universally worshiped in all of the different *poleis* (city states). Apollo is the god of the sun, medicine, music and poetry, prophecy, and truth, and is the protector of young boys. Apollo was also considered a patron of men who love men, and myths describe him taking many, many lovers, including both men and women. The fact that one of the most popular gods was so explicitly queer speaks to how accepted queer men were in Hellenic society.

Like Apollo, Dionysus is also associated with men who love men and is described taking both male and female lovers. Unlike Apollo, Dionysus and his worshipers were viewed with suspicion or even fear by mainstream society.

Dionysus is associated with wine, sex, madness, strangers, and those outside of society. His worship included both orgies and human sacrifices. He was sometimes associated with the Underworld, and his worship was especially popular with women and marginalized people.

Even Dionysus's birth is explicitly queer. Dionysus's mother was murdered while she was pregnant with him. To save the unborn god, his father Zeus placed the fetus inside his own body and gave birth to Dionysus himself.

Some myths say Dionysus was raised as a girl until adulthood, and as an adult he is depicted as very androgynous in art. Dionysus was associated with aspects of queerness that were seen as taboo in Hellenic society.

While Dionysus was and is popular with queer women, the most well-known Hellenic patroness of queer women is Artemis. Artemis is Apollo's twin sister and is associated with the moon, hunting, wilderness, childbirth, and virginity. Artemis is also the protector of young girls. Like Apollo, she was widely worshiped.

It is important to note that in Hellenic culture, a virgin was any woman who had never had sex with a man, which included women who only had sex with women. Artemis never married. She spent her time roaming the wilds with her hunters, who were all women. As with Nephthys, scholars debate whether Artemis was originally understood to be a lesbian. On one hand, a woman rejecting marriage and domestic life and choosing to surround herself exclusively with women does sound gay. On the other hand, there are no surviving sources that explicitly say Artemis took women as lovers. The academic debate around this goddess's orientation is centuries-old, and it will probably never be settled unless new evidence is found. Whether or not she was originally associated with women who love women, the queer community has long claimed Artemis as one of its patron deities. For thousands of years, queer women have resonated with this fierce, independent goddess.

In the 1960s and 1970s, feminists and lesbian activists used symbols of Artemis and her Roman counterpart, Diana, to tie their political movement into the history of queer womanhood. While we may never know if her original worshipers saw Artemis as a queer woman, she is definitely a goddess of modern queer activism.

One Hellenic goddess who *was* explicitly associated with lesbians is Aphrodite. Sappho, the poet from whom we get the terms "lesbian" and "sapphic," was a devotee of Aphrodite and called her the patron of love between women. Other sources say that Aphrodite is the patron of all same-sex relationships. As the goddess of love and sex, it seems she didn't discriminate when bestowing her blessing on loving couples.

Aphrodite is also associated with intersex and nonbinary identities. The Roman author Macrobius described a version of Aphrodite with a beard and a penis who was worshiped in Cyprus. Some statues of this "Aphroditus" have survived to the modern day. Statues depict Aphrodite as a beautiful woman in feminine clothing, lifting up her skirts to reveal her erect penis. Rituals worshiping this intersex aspect of Aphrodite involved men and women trading clothing.

Hellenic paganism also has explicit examples of binary transgender identities (i.e., male-to-female or female-to-male). One of these is Caeneus. Originally a female nymph named Caenis, he became a lover of the god Poseidon. Poseidon was so impressed by his lover that he offered to grant any wish Caeneus might have. Caeneus wished for a male body, which Poseidon granted.

Queer Gods of the Roman Pantheon

The Roman pantheon shares some overlap with the Hellenic pantheon. Some Hellenic gods, like Apollo and Dionysus/ Bacchus were adopted by the Romans and stayed very similar to their Hellenic forms. Others, like Artemis and Aphrodite, were syncretized with existing Latin or Etruscan deities to become part of a larger whole. Images and stories of Artemis were incorporated into worship of the goddess Diana and images and stories of Aphrodite were incorporated into the worship of the goddess Venus.

These deities mostly kept their queer associations. For example, my partner and I invoked Venus Aphroditus ("Venus Who Is Aphroditus") in our Roman pagan wedding ceremony.

Rome also produced its own stories of queer deities. These stories show differences in Hellenic and Roman values, including differences in how queer identity was viewed by these cultures.

Mars, the patron god of Rome and one of the most important gods in the state religion, was said by some Romans to have two mothers. The Roman author Ovid wrote that the goddess Juno became jealous when her husband Jupiter gave birth to the goddess Minerva from his mind, cutting Juno (his wife and the goddess of childbirth) out of the birthing process. Juno sought out Flora, the goddess of flowers and vegetation, to help her birth her own child without a man. Flora used a magical flower to impregnate Juno, who later gave birth to Mars.

The story of Mars's birth highlights how valued motherhood was in Roman culture. In many ways, Mars was the archetype of the perfect Roman man. Unlike his Hellenic counterpart, Ares, Mars was stately, dignified, and responsible. He was the model Roman citizens aspired to live up to.

The fact that many Romans believed Mars was born of two women shows that, to them, a father wasn't necessarily a requirement for a good moral upbringing. We can compare this to how the Romans viewed Bachus, who had a father but no mother and was seen as a god of depravity.

Later influences from the Middle East would introduce a class of third gender priests to the Roman state religion. When the Phrygian goddess Cybele was officially added to the Roman pantheon during the Second Punic War, she brought her genderbending priests with her.

The *galli* (singular *gallus)* were human servants of the goddess who were often castrated men and who dressed in women's clothing. The galli were also associated with gay sex and were part of a tradition of third gender priesthood dating back to the worship of the Sumerian goddess Inanna.

Cybele wasn't the only Eastern god to find favor with transgender and nonbinary people in Rome. The Arabic sun god Elagabal was the patron deity of the emperor Elagabalus. Elagabalus was a high priest of Elagabal before becoming the emperor of Rome and brought the sun god with her when she took control of the empire.

Widely considered a transgender woman by modern scholars, Elagabalus was born male but presented as feminine and famously offered a reward to any doctor who could give her a vagina. She may have found solace in the priesthood of Elagabal, which was similar to the galli and would have been a safe haven for gender-nonconforming Romans.

Elagabalus was an unpopular emperor, partly because of her gender identity and partly because of her devotion to a non-Roman god. However, she was successful in bringing Elagabal's worship to Rome by syncretizing him with the Roman sun god, Sol.

Sol was previously an obscure deity, but after taking on Elagabal's fierceness he became known as Sol Invictus ("The Unconquered Sun") and became an important part of the imperial religion. The worship of Sol Invictus would forever change Roman religious life, and would even go on to influence early Christianity.

Queer Gods of the Norse Pantheon

Outside of the Mediterranean, surviving references to queer gods are less common. This may not be because other Western cultures didn't value queer people. In fact, some Germanic and Celtic groups may have recognized same-sex unions as being similar to a marriage between a man and a woman. These cultures just left less complete records of all aspects of their religion. We know less about their queer gods because we know less about all of their gods.

This doesn't necessarily mean they were homophobic or transphobic. It just means we don't have many clear records of their beliefs. In some cases, references to same-sex relationships and nonbinary gender may have been intentionally destroyed by later Christians who saw these stories as sinful. Luckily, a few examples of queer deities from Northern, Central, and Eastern Europe have survived.

One of the most well-known genderqueer deities in modern pop culture is Loki, a trickster deity worshiped by the Norse. Loki is a complex and often misunderstood figure. They are the sworn blood-brother of Odin, the chief of the main tribe of Norse gods, and frequently travel with Thor. At the same time, Loki is the parent of fearsome monsters and orchestrated the murder of the beloved god Baldr. It doesn't help that the Christian scribes who recorded most of our surviving Norse myths related Loki to the Devil. It can be difficult to step away from dualistic, good vs. evil thinking and see Loki in all their nuance.

Loki's main role is as a force of change. Their purpose is to challenge those in authority and to shake up the status quo. This change is sometimes uncomfortable or even painful, but it can also bring great blessings.

Loki is not any more evil than a forest fire, though both can cause destruction. Folklore, linguistics, and place names indicate that Loki was worshiped alongside the other Norse gods, so they clearly weren't seen as evil by the pagan Norse people.

Loki has the ability to shapeshift, which they often use to change their sex. In at least one myth, Loki turns into a female animal and gives birth. They are also described as fathering several children, and as taking the form of an old woman. Loki's relationship with gender is clearly very fluid, and their subversion of Norse masculinity is often highlighted in the myths.

While less obviously queer than Loki, the god Odin also subverts masculinity.

To modern readers of Norse myths, Odin may seem very masculine. He is the chief of the Aesir, the main tribe of Norse gods. He is a warrior and a father to many children. He was historically worshiped by warriors and kings. Pop culture has taken this vision of Odin and run with it, making him into a stern, strict father figure.

But Odin is also a trickster with a feminine side. Like Loki, Odin often visits humans to cause mischief or conflict. Like Loki, Odin changes his shape and sometimes takes on the shape of a woman. Both Odin and Loki are associated with cunning and with tricks.

Odin is also the god of *seidr*, a Norse magical practice that was seen as feminine. While Odin boasts about his knowledge of *galdr*, the more masculine Norse word-magic, he also explicitly practices seidr in the myths.

We know that men who practiced seidr faced a social stigma and were sometimes accused of being gay. Those same accusations are made against both Odin and Loki in surviving Norse literature. It is clear that Odin was understood as subverting gender and sexuality norms in Norse society, even if this subversion isn't clear to modern readers.

Connecting with Deity

There are many, many more queer deities than I am able to mention here, and I encourage you to do your own research. I hope this brief discussion has made it clear that queerness has always had a place in spirituality and that there are deities out there who understand our experiences as modern queer people. We all deserve to see ourselves in the gods we worship.

And, of course, there are many, many, many deities who may not be associated with queerness but who seem more than willing to connect with queer worshipers. Many queer witches, myself included, work with deities that aren't explicitly connected to queer identity and still find our identities affirmed and uplifted by those relationships.

For most of the years I have been a witch, the main deity I work with has been the Norse goddess Freyja. As far as I am aware, there are no Norse sources linking Freyja to queer identity. And yet, I experience her as a goddess of womanhood beyond uteruses and vaginas, who loves and protects all women no matter their sex assigned at birth. I experience her as a goddess of all love and all healthy, consensual sex, no matter the number, gender, or orientation of the people involved. I experience her as a goddess who loves me in my queerness and who pushes me to live as my authentic self. My years-long relationship with Freyja brings joy and meaning to my life, and I want more queer people to experience that kind of loving relationship with the divine.

If you feel a pull toward any of the gods mentioned in this book, or some other deity you discovered somewhere else, I encourage you to follow it. Read their stories. Look at images of them created by the culture that first honored them. Speak to people who work with them, either in person or online. Think about whether this is someone you would like to have a relationship with. Because that is what worship is, at the end of the day: a relationship.

If you feel ready to take the next step, invite your deity in for a small, private moment to get to know each other.

This can be as simple as sitting quietly alone and opening yourself up to their presence, but candles are nice if you have them. Make a small offering – water, coffee, or tea is just fine. If you feel more comfortable with a more structured meeting, you can use tarot or oracle cards or another divination tool to have a conversation with the deity.

Talk to them, either out loud or in your head. These don't have to be formal prayers, but they can be if you feel called to that. Ask this deity what they want from a relationship with you, and what they are offering in return. Ask them how they would like for you to honor them. Get to know each other.

Remember, relationships with deities are a lot like our relationships with other humans. And just like in human relationships, you always have the right to say no or to end the relationship. You don't have to worship any deity if you don't want to. You don't even have to call what you do worship if that makes you uncomfortable. You have autonomy to make your own decisions.

One of the things I find liberating about polytheism, or working with many gods, is knowing that my relationships with deities can and should change. Some are constants, like my relationship with Freyja. Others wax and wane, with gods coming into my life for a few weeks or months and then leaving, only to return after a long absence and start the cycle over again. Sometimes I find myself working with a deity on a specific project, like a book I'm writing or a ritual I'm hosting, and then they move on when the project is completed. Sometimes I work with a deity closely for months or years, and then we drift apart until I realize one day that they no longer have a place in my practice. All of this is healthy and natural.

Your relationship with the divine, if you choose to have one, is entirely up to you. Only you can decide what is right for your worship of the deities you choose.

Chapter 9

A Queer Wheel of the Year

Everyone loves a good party. No matter who we are or what we believe, taking time to celebrate life with the people we love is important. Holidays are set days of the year when we take a break from the grind for some life-affirming celebration.

Queer witchcraft has no set calendar of holidays. However, there are some sacred days that are very popular with queer witches, in addition to any other religious, cultural, or secular holidays they may celebrate. This set of witchy holidays is called the Wheel of the Year, and it is the focus of this chapter. In Chapter 10, we will discuss how to craft rituals for secular holidays and create your own holiday calendar.

The modern Wheel of the Year comes from Wicca, but it is by no means exclusive to Wiccans. Many non-Wiccan witches choose to work with at least some of the holidays on the Wheel, and the holidays themselves date back to pre-Christian festivals from Western Europe, particularly England, Scotland, Ireland, and Wales. The Wheel of the Year is even used by some atheist and agnostic witches as a way of connecting with the rhythms and cycles of the natural world.

Because of their popularity with a variety of witches and pagans, many major cities have public celebrations for the holidays on the Wheel, which can be great opportunities to make like-minded friends.

The Wheel of the Year has eight "spokes", the eight holidays sometimes called *sabbats*. The Wheel is a solar calendar and is deeply connected to the relationship between the Sun and the Earth. The Wheel of the Year combines the Germanic celebration of the solstices and equinoxes with four Gaelic fire festivals. These holidays have roots in ancient times.

Some of the sabbats incorporate Roman and/or Norse traditions. This is because England, where Wicca was founded, has a complex history of religious and historical influences. Before the conversion to Christianity, religion in Britain was a mix of Anglo-Saxon and Celtic practices, with some less prominent Roman and Norse influences. Folk magic in England reflected these mixed cultural influences, and so does the Wheel of the Year.

The dates on the Wheel of the Year are based on the progression of the seasons in the Northern hemisphere, and specifically in Western Europe. Witches in the Southern hemisphere often reverse the dates of the sabbats to better match their local seasons – so while witches in the Northern hemisphere are celebrating the summer solstice, witches in the Southern hemisphere celebrate the winter solstice. I give the dates for both hemispheres in this chapter.

There is no requirement to celebrate the Wheel of the Year to be a witch. This holiday calendar may or may not resonate with you, and that's okay. Feel free to only celebrate the holidays that interest you, or to ignore the Wheel entirely. I include them here because they are the holidays you are most likely to see other witches celebrating, but that doesn't mean you have to include them in your practice.

Because of the Wheel of the Year's British roots, some witches choose to use a holiday calendar that is more culturally relevant to them. You might choose to focus only on the Wheel of the Year, to combine it with holidays from your own culture(s), or to ignore it entirely. Only you can decide what is right for your practice.

The information given on the sabbats in this chapter is meant as a jumping off point for creating your own celebrations. We'll start with Yule, the winter solstice, when the old year dies and the new year is born.

Yule

Dates: December 21-22 in the Northern hemisphere, June 20-21 in the Southern hemisphere
Also Called: Winter Solstice, Midwinter
Theme: Birth of the Divine Child

Yule is the time of birth. The two previous sabbats, the Fall Equinox and Samhain, are connected to themes of death and the Underworld. At Yule, our focus shifts to rebirth and new life. The previous year "dies" and the new year is "born."

The winter solstice marks the shortest day and longest night of the year. Astronomically, the Earth's pole is tilted away from the sun, and as a result the sun appears at its lowest point in the sky. This is technically the first day of winter, although many of us have already been experiencing darkness and cold weather for several weeks on this date. For this reason, this solstice is sometimes called "Midwinter."

At Yule, darkness triumphs over light and night triumphs over day. It is literally the darkest day of the year. Darkness and night are not bad or scary – in fact, they are a deeply necessary part of life. At Yule, we celebrate the dark night as a time of peaceful rest. At the same time, we welcome back the light and warmth, which will begin to return after this solstice. Yule marks the end of the "dark half" of the year and the beginning of the "light half."

Yule is all about new beginnings and fresh starts. This is the time to lay to rest the stresses and troubles of the past year and prepare ourselves for new things. This is also a powerful time of year for self-reflection, maybe even with help from a divination tool like tarot cards or a pendulum.

The energy of Yule is connected to the Birth of the Divine Child. This motif deals with the birth or rebirth of a sacred being and appears in religion and folklore from all over the world. It can be found in Egyptian stories of the birth of Horus, ancient Roman stories of the birth of Sol Invictus, Buddhist stories of the conception and birth of the Buddha, and Christian stories of the virgin birth of Jesus. In some European cultures, the birth of the Divine Child is connected to the return of the summer sun, which is "born" on the winter solstice.

While birth is sometimes seen as something only for cisgender, heterosexual people, many myths tell birth stories that break this mold. The Greek father god Zeus gave birth to two of his children: Athena, who was born from his skull, and Dionysus, who was born from his thigh. Mars, the patron god of Rome, was conceived when the goddess Juno was impregnated by the goddess Flora. The Norse god Loki both fathered and gave birth to children.

These stories remind us that each pregnancy and birth is unique, and that birth is not restricted to any one gender or orientation. They also remind us that queer and trans parents have been around for a very, very long time.

Yule is a time to welcome in the things we wish to birth in the new year, and to celebrate the relationships, families, and communities that bring us joy. It is a very festive holiday, with celebrations that literally bring light to the darkest night of the year. Yule has the energy of sitting around the fire with people you love and trust, singing songs and telling stories.

There is some overlap between Yule traditions and Christmas traditions. Things like lighting candles on the nights leading up to the solstice, bringing evergreen trees or wreaths into the home, and exchanging gifts are all part of both Christmas and Yule.

Sacred space for Yule features many symbols that may seem familiar to anyone who has celebrated Christmas. The space is decorated with boughs of evergreen and mistletoe, possibly even including a tree or a Yule log. Candles and other lights also play a big part in Yule decorations. You could also include an image of the divine infant and/or the sun. Colors associated with Yule are green, red, white, and gold.

Imbolc

Dates: February 1 in the Northern hemisphere, August 1 in the Southern hemisphere
Also Called: Imbolg, Brigid's Day, Candlemas
Theme: Nurturing

Imbolc is the first Gaelic holiday of the year. At Imbolc, it is still winter, but we can see the first signs of spring beginning to appear. The days are getting lighter, and we know spring is just around the corner. In agrarian cultures, this is the time of year when ewes (female sheep) start producing milk.

Historically, Imbolc was observed by lighting candles to celebrate the increased sunlight as winter came to an end. This is where an alternative name for the holiday, Candlemas (literally "candle mass") comes from. Modern Imbolc celebrations still often include lots of candles and other types of lights.

Historically, this was also a time for ritual purification with blessed water or a sacred candle flame, which prepared the household and the fields for the coming planting season. Even today, rituals for this sabbat tend to be focused on purification and blessing.

This focus on purification at the beginning of February was also present in ancient Rome – the word "February" comes from the Latin *februa*, meaning "purification." The *Februa* or *Februalia* was a Roman festival dedicated to ritual purification, especially purification with fire.

Because of this connection to fire, the Februalia was connected to the Roman hearth goddess, Vesta. We still see this focus on hearth and home in modern Imbolc celebrations. It's a sabbat for homebodies, with a focus on sharing light and warmth with our loved ones.

In Celtic countries, Imbolc is associated with the goddess Bríg (also called Brigid, Brigit, or Brid). Bríg is one of a few pan-Celtic deities, and she was worshiped in some form by nearly every culture under the Celtic umbrella, both in the isles and on the continent.

Bríg was so beloved that after the conversion to Christianity, many of her myths were incorporated into the figure of Saint Brigid of Kildare. Saint Brigid is still considered a saint by the Catholic Church, and her feast day falls on February 1 and incorporates many traditional Imbolc celebrations.

Bríg/Brigid is the goddess/patron saint of foster mothers, and this aspect of her is emphasized at Imbolc. This side of Bríg is especially relevant for queer people, as we may find ourselves raising or caring for children we did not birth ourselves. One of Bríg's lessons is that parenthood doesn't have to live up to our culture's stereotypes to be valid.

This goddess and saint is associated with both fire and water, the two means of purification at Imbolc. In Gaelic cultures, families would invite her into the home and ask her blessing on the household. Many modern witches and pagans still honor Bríg on Imbolc.

The energy of Imbolc is very gentle and uplifting, with themes of nurturing, caregiving, bringing light into the darkness, and hope for spring. This is a day to spend cozied up with the people you love, showing them how much they mean to you. It is also a day to check in with yourself and make sure your own physical and emotional needs are being taken care of.

Sacred space for Imbolc celebrations usually features lots of candles. Gold or yellow candles are especially appropriate, as they represent the returning sun. You might also include traditional symbols like the Brigid's cross or sun cross, a cross or "X" shape woven from straw with a diamond shape where the arms of the cross meet. The colors commonly associated with Imbolc are white, red, yellow, and green.

Spring Equinox

Dates: March 20-23 in the Northern hemisphere, September 20-23 in the Southern hemisphere
Also Called: Ostara, Eostre, The Rites of Spring
Theme: The Dying and Rising Deity

This equinox is the first official day of spring, although those of us living in warmer climates may feel the arrival of spring several weeks earlier.

In my area, this is the time when dandelions and violets are popping up everywhere I look, and if I'm lucky I may see baby animals enjoying the warm weather with their parents. The world is waking up after the long, dark days of winter, and the air sings with joy and potential.

This is definitely a time of fertility, but we should remember that fertility is about much more than just the literal conception and birth of children. (Although, if you were thinking about doing some magic for a pregnancy, adoption, surrogacy, or IVF cycle, now would be an excellent time for it!)

For those who are a little uncomfortable with talk of fertilized wombs, it can be helpful instead to think of fertility in the agricultural sense. The land is said to be fertile when it can support life – when newly planted seeds have everything they need to grow. Our lives are like that rich, fertile soil, and the spring equinox is a great time to think about the things we want to "plant" in our lives. This is a wonderful time to start new projects or endeavors.

At the spring and fall equinoxes, daytime and nighttime are exactly equal. This only happens twice a year! Balance is a key theme on both of these days. The equinoxes serve as a reminder that, in nature, perfect balance is actually very rare. And because balance is so rare, the equinoxes are powerful days for magic and ritual.

The energy of the spring equinox is connected to the motif of the Dying and Rising Deity. This is a religious motif in which a god or goddess dies before returning to life. The Dying and Rising Deity is found in many cultures across the world, such as in stories of Dumuzi in ancient Sumer, Osiris in ancient Egypt, Persephone in ancient Greece, Baldr in pre-Christian Scandinavia, and yes, Jesus Christ in Christianity.

The motif of the Dying and Rising Deity is closely related to the motif of the Descent into the Underworld. For example, the myth of Persephone's abduction by Hades could be understood either as a cycle of death and resurrection or as a descent and return from the Underworld, depending on how you interpret the ancient texts.

Myths of Dying and Rising Deities usually revolve around agricultural deities. For example, in Ancient Egypt, the death and resurrection of Osiris was connected to the planting and sprouting of grain. Planting seeds was seen as a symbolic burial of the great god, and the sprouting plants were seen as proof of his resurrection. Many other deities associated with this motif, like Persephone and Baldr, are also associated with plant life.

In Western cultures, this connection between the Dying and Rising Deity and the Spring Equinox survives in yearly Easter celebrations. Originally a Christian holiday based on the older Jewish feast of Passover, Easter marks the resurrection of Jesus Christ after his death.

Modern Easter celebrations include colorful eggs, which may be a symbol of rebirth. The egg holds the potential of new life, and the lovely pastel colors remind us of the flowers and young plants that mark the beginning of spring.

Sacred space for Spring Equinox celebrations is decorated with as many different types and colors of flowers as you can get your hands on. You can also include dyed eggs, and maybe even decorate them with your favorite symbols of rebirth and transformation. The colors commonly associated with this equinox are springtime pastels, especially green, pink, yellow, and white.

May Day

Dates: May 1 in the Northern hemisphere, November 1 in the Southern hemisphere
Also Called: Beltane, Bealtaine, Walpurgisnacht, the Floralia
Theme: The Trickster

While the Spring Equinox marks the beginning of spring, May Day marks its peak. By this time of year, the days are warm and sunny, plant and animal life are abundant, and summer feels right around the corner. (For those of us living in warmer climates, it may feel like summer already has one foot in the door.)

Like Imbolc, May Day has its roots in Gaelic traditions. It is sometimes called Bealtaine (pronounced "b-YEL-ten-uh") in Irish or Beltane ("BEL-tane") in English.

Bealtaine sits opposite the wheel from Samhain, another Gaelic festival, and the two have some important parallels. Like Samhain, Bealtaine is known as a time when the veil between the worlds is thin, allowing easier connections between humans and spirits.

The category of Otherworld spirits most strongly associated with Bealtaine is the Fairies, respectfully referred to with euphemisms like The Good People or The Other Crowd. Many Bealtaine traditions in Ireland and Scotland are centered on honoring the Good People to gain their blessing and, more importantly, avoid falling victim to their mischief.

At its heart, May Day/Bealtaine is a fire festival. The word "Bealtaine" may be connected to the concept of lucky fire, and the festival is traditionally celebrated in Ireland with bonfires. (These were historically true bone-fires, with the bones of animals used as fuel for the fire.)

Many of the oldest Bealtaine rituals involve using fire for blessings and protection. There is an old folk practice in Ireland of building two bonfires and driving livestock between them to bless the animals and protect them from disease. Author Morgan Daimler describes a practice in which the head of the family lights a candle and uses it to bless the door, the four corners of the home, and each family member in turn. I personally feel that fire is an essential part of the spirit of this holiday and make sure to always include real flames in my celebrations, even if all I can do is light a small candle.

Flowers play a large part in both Gaelic Bealtaine and British May Day celebrations, as well as a related Roman festival, the *Floralia*. "Bringing in the May," or bringing fresh spring flowers into the home to bring blessings and good luck, is a time honored tradition throughout England, Scotland, and Ireland. Flowers are also used for personal decoration and as gifts for loved ones.

The energy of May Day is connected to the Trickster archetype. The Trickster is an enigmatic figure, often hard to pin down. The Trickster exists to defy the mainstream social order by subverting the normal manner of things and refusing to follow the rules society has set out for them. They may seem to create chaos as a result of their actions, but the Trickster has the very important purpose of keeping the social order in check by reminding us all how fragile it really is. Often, the Trickster is a catalyst for needed change.

The Trickster archetype is embodied by deities such as the Hellenic Hermes, the Chinese Sun Wukong, and the Norse Loki. Even deities we don't often think of as Tricksters can sometimes take on this role, such as when the Sumerian goddess, Inanna, got her father, Ea, drunk and tricked him into giving her the *me* (the skills that make civilization possible).

The Good People, who play a central role in Gaelic Bealtaine lore, can be considered a culture of tricksters. Fairy operates on its own rules, which can sometimes seem like an inversion of our own. When the Good People appear in myth and folklore, it is often to teach a lesson by inflicting chaos and mischief on people who don't abide by their rules. Bealtaine rituals and celebrations honor the important social role of these tricksters, while also taking steps to stay on their good side and protect ourselves from their mischief.

May 1 is also the feast day of the Christian Saint Walpurga. In Germany and some other European countries, *Walpurgisnacht,* the night before Saint Wulpurga's Day, is celebrated with bonfires that are said to protect against witches and evil spirits.

In Ancient Rome, this time of year was marked by the Floralia, a feast honoring the goddess Flora. During the Floralia, people celebrated with sexual innuendos and lighthearted games.

Historic May Day festivities in England included erecting large wooden stakes called maypoles and dancing around them with colored ribbons so that the ribbons were wound around the pole. A young woman from the community might be crowned May Queen, and a man dressed as the enigmatic Green Man might lead a parade.

Traditional British May Day celebrations have a flirtatious vibe, with young people pairing up at maypole dances and possibly beginning a courtship. Some celebrations involve kissing, although this isn't necessarily sensual kissing, since children also sometimes participate. In other places, May Day has taken on an explicitly sexual aspect.

Queer people face a lot of pressure to sanitize our romantic experiences for public consumption. To push back against homophobic and transphobic claims that our identities are deviant or perverse, we've learned to present only the most squeaky-clean, wholesome, sexless versions of ourselves in public. We avoid even suggesting that queer people are sexual beings. Many queer people feel uncomfortable even kissing their partner(s) in public for fear of being shamed or harassed.

Even in designated queer spaces, sex is often downplayed or limited to late-night "adults-only" events.

For queer witches, May Day is a yearly reminder that our sexual needs and desires are sacred and worthy of being celebrated. It can be an opportunity to try something new in the bedroom, with our partner(s) or on our own. It can give us a chance to rediscover what we like and what makes us feel good. It can also be a time to reevaluate our relationship with sex. Even for asexual and celibate witches, May Day can be a powerful time to reaffirm that not having sex can be an equally empowering choice.

If you choose to incorporate sexual elements or themes into your May Day celebrations, you must make informed consent your top priority. The easiest way to bring sex into ritual is to plan a private, intimate ritual for just yourself or just you and your partner(s).

If you are choosing to celebrate with other witches, such as with a coven, make sure everyone who will be participating is involved in planning the ritual and establishing the group's comfort zone. Make sure each participant knows that they can stop at any time, and give people the option to sit out parts of the ritual they aren't personally comfortable participating in.

Some elements of sexuality and nudity, such as going *skyclad* (naked) or physically touching other participants, should only be done if the group unanimously agrees that they feel comfortable including them. Needless to say, any ritual containing nudity or sexual themes should be strictly adults-only and invitation-only. Rituals that are open to the public are not the place to start experimenting with sacred sexuality.

If you decide to plan a ritual with sexual themes, be mindful of the identities of the people you will be sharing sacred space with. If several of your covenmates are queer, it would be tone deaf and alienating to focus only on heterosexual sexuality in your ritual.

Use your creativity and do a little research to make sure all participants feel that their sexuality is being celebrated. Include myths and stories of queer lovers like Gilgamesh and Enkidu, Apollo and Hyacinthus, or Athena and Myrmex. Affirm that all loving sexual partnerships are sacred, regardless of the gender or anatomy of the people involved.

If the theme of sacred sexuality does not resonate with you right now, you do not have to include it in your May Day celebrations. You can work with the Trickster archetype and the magic of springtime, which will make for a wonderful and meaningful celebration all on their own.

Sacred space for May Day celebrations is decorated with fresh, seasonal flowers, much like the Spring Equinox. If you are mainly drawing from Gaelic traditions, you might include yellow flowers, which are believed to bring blessings in Irish lore. Otherwise, any and all colored blooms are welcome.

You might include a maypole – this can be anything from a living tree to a small wooden dowel, with colorful ribbons tied around the top. Like the Spring Equinox, May Day is associated with pastel yellow and pink, but it is also associated with deep, rich shades of green and sometimes red. The most important part of your May Day decor is your sacred fire, whether it takes the form of a small candle or a roaring bonfire.

Summer Solstice

Dates: June 20-21 in the Northern hemisphere, December 21-22 in the Southern hemisphere
Also Called: Midsummer, Litha
Theme: The Sacred Marriage

The Summer Solstice marks the longest day and shortest night of the year. Astronomically, the earth's pole is tilted towards the sun, and as a result the sun appears at its highest point in the sky. This is technically the first day of summer, but in many warmer climates summer is well underway by the end of June – hence the term "Midsummer."

At the Summer Solstice, light triumphs over dark and day triumphs over night. It is quite literally the lightest day of the year. And yet, after this solstice, the days begin to shorten as we move into the "dark half" of the year. The solstice is both a celebration of the light and warmth at their height and a time to welcome the returning dark and cold, which will bring the harvest and the rest and introspection of winter.

The fertility themes of the Spring Equinox and May Day shift to a focus on abundance at the Summer Solstice. We are no longer dealing with just the potential for life and growth – growth is now happening all around us, and we can see it in the natural world. This solstice is a time to give thanks for the abundance already present in our lives, whether a literal abundant crop in your personal garden, financial abundance, an abundance of joy and love, or some other area of your life that is especially plentiful right now.

The energy of the Summer Solstice is connected to the archetype of the Sacred Marriage. This religious motif deals with the union of two or more complementary forces, often represented in myths with the marriage of two gods. This is one of the oldest mythic archetypes. It can be found in *The Courtship of Inanna and Dumuzi*, a Sumerian poem that has survived to this day. Other examples include Isis and Osiris in Ancient Egypt, Zeus and Hera in Ancient Greece, and the Morrigan and the Dagda in Irish mythology.

Although we use the term "marriage," not all examples of this archetype involve a literal wedding or married couple. The energy of the Sacred Marriage is present any time two or more people choose to share their lives and resources in a loving union. This includes opposite-sex couples that are not married, such as the Greek Aphrodite and Ares. It also includes same-sex couples, such as the Babylonian Gilgamesh and Enkidu, and polyamorous relationships such as the Greek Achilles, Patroclus, and Briseis. The Sacred Marriage is a celebration of love, connection, and cooperation. While this is often expressed in myths as a marriage or a romantic affair, it can also show up in family and/or platonic relationships.

Throughout the world, complementary forces of nature are associated with divine siblings such as the Greek sun god Apollo and moon goddess Artemis, the Norse fertility god Freyr and fertility goddess Freyja, and the Fon creator goddess Mawu and her brother Lisa. These sibling relationships are just as important and worthy of celebration as relationships between romantic partners, and choosing to focus on myths about platonic relationships in your solstice rituals can make them more accessible for asexual and aromantic people.

The Summer Solstice is a time to celebrate not only the love between the gods, but also our own loving relationships. It's convenient that the solstice falls during June, which is celebrated as LGBTQ+ Pride Month in the United States and many other countries. Celebrations of queer love, friendship, and found family are absolutely in keeping with the spirit of the solstice.

The Sun features heavily in Summer Solstice lore and celebrations, and this is reflected in sacred space for this sabbat. You might consider making an image of the Sun the central focus of your solstice decorations. You can also include images of embracing couples, happy families, and/or friends enjoying each other's company. You may also include summer greenery. The colors commonly associated with this solstice are gold, yellow, orange, and red.

Lammas

Dates: August 1 in the Northern hemisphere, February 1 in the Southern hemisphere

Also Called: Lughnasa

Theme: The Harvest

Lammas, also called Lughnasa (pronounced "loo-NAW-saw," also spelled Lughnasadh or Lunasa) is another Gaelic holiday. Lammas comes from an Old English word meaning "loaf mass," and is connected to the harvest of grain. The other name for the holiday, Lughnasa, comes from the name of the Irish god Lugh. Throughout England, Ireland, and Scotland, Lughnasa/Lammas was historically celebrated with grain-based foods like bread and porridge.

Lammas marks the beginning of autumn or, more accurately, the harvest season. While many of us may still be experiencing summer weather at this time of year, this is also when autumn produce begins to be ready for harvest. This is a time to appreciate the abundance of the harvest and begin preparing for the colder months ahead.

Lammas sits across the Wheel from Imbolc, and these two holidays can be seen as mirror images of each other. At Imbolc, we celebrate light and warmth in the dark half of the year and prepare for the coming spring. At Lammas, we celebrate the lingering warmth of summer and prepare for the coming winter. While Imbolc is often celebrated indoors around the hearth, Lammas is best celebrated outdoors whenever possible.

The Irish name of this holiday translates to "funeral assembly of Lugh" in Old Irish, referencing the belief that Lugh created the festival to honor his deceased foster-mother, Tailtiu. Despite this, Lughnasa is a very fun and joyous holiday and was historically celebrated in Ireland with harvest festivals and athletic competitions.

The energy of Lammas is all about the harvest. Lammas celebrations are about spending time with people you love, enjoying beautiful summer weather, and eating lots of good food. On a deeper level, this is a chance to give thanks to the land for feeding and nurturing us and to honor spirits and deities associated with the harvest.

Harvest deities are often some of the most beloved of any pantheon – after all, we all need to eat, and we tend to like the people who keep us fed. Deities associated with the harvest tend to also be connected to hospitality, abundance, and plenty. For example, in Irish lore the Dagda is said to own a cauldron that can never be emptied, and it is said that no one who eats from this cauldron goes away unsatisfied. The Norse sibling deities Freyr and Freyja are both associated with the harvest and with love and pleasure. In many Native American cultures, corn or maize is personified as a deity who feeds and teaches the people, such as the Maize Woman of Maya mythology or Selu, the Cherokee corn mother. Harvest deities remind us that food is deeply connected to community and family.

This connection between food and family can be seen in the tradition of Lughnasa handfasting. In Ireland and Scotland, this was the traditional time of year for handfasting and weddings. On Lughnasa, couples could enter a "trial marriage" in which they would live together as a married couple for one year before deciding whether to continue the union. At the following year's Lughnasa festival, they could either choose to renew their marriage and make it permanent or walk away without any legal penalty.

If you or someone you know is planning a wedding, Lammas/ Lughnasa would be an appropriate time for it. There is some evidence that some Celtic cultures recognized same sex unions as being similar to a marriage, so queer Lammas weddings are absolutely also appropriate.

Lammas is a time to express our gratitude, not only for the food we eat, but for all the blessings in our lives. It is a time especially to acknowledge and celebrate the fruits of our own labor, whether literal or metaphorical. If you worked hard to earn a promotion at your job, or spent hours of your free time working on a creative project, or finally saved up enough to take that vacation you've been dreaming of, these are the result of "seeds" you have planted and tended to. This is a great time to celebrate your wins from the previous year, big or small.

Sacred space for Lammas celebrations incorporates lots of harvest imagery, especially images of grain. Fill your working space with ears of corn, sheaves of wheat, or any other grains you can get your hands on. You could also include symbols associated with the harvest, such as a sickle and pitch fork (or miniature versions of these tools, if you are working indoors). Colors associated with Lammas are gold, deep yellow, orange, and red.

Fall Equinox

Dates: September 21-23 in the Northern hemisphere, March 20-23 in the Southern hemisphere
Also Called: Autumn Equinox, Mabon
Theme: Descent into the Underworld

This equinox is the first official day of fall – although if you live in a colder climate, it may feel like fall has arrived long before the end of September! In my area, this is the time when the leaves on the trees are beginning to turn to brilliant reds and yellows. The days are getting shorter, the weather is getting colder, and the chill in the air carries the promise of the coming winter.

Like the spring equinox, the fall equinox is one of only two dates in the year when day and night are exactly equal. Because of this balance between day and night, light and dark, balance in general is a key theme of this sabbat.

The autumn equinox is a good time to take a step back, look at our lives, and see if we can make things a little more balanced. If you've been putting in a lot of overtime at work, now would be a good time to take some time off to spend with loved ones. If you've been spending a lot of time alone, try to schedule something fun with friends. If there is an area of life you've been ignoring because you don't want to deal with it (household chores and mental health care both often get this treatment), the autumn equinox is a great time to face that task head on.

The energy of the fall equinox is connected to the myth of the Descent Into the Underworld. Similar to the myth of the Dying and Rising Deity we celebrated at the spring equinox, the Descent deals with an actual journey into the land of the dead. The Ancient Greeks actually had a special word for this mythic archetype: *katabasis.*

One of the oldest versions of this motif appears in the story of Inanna's Descent, a Sumerian myth in which the goddess Inanna, the Queen of Heaven (later called Ishtar by the Assyrians and Babylonians) goes to the land of the dead to visit her sister Ereshkigal, Queen of the Dead. This motif also appears in other myths from cultures all over the world, such as the Ancient Greek tale of Orpheus and Eurydice, the Welsh god Pwyll's journey to Annwn (the Otherworld), and the Japanese god Izanagi going into the land of the dead to look for his wife, Izanami.

As we noted in our discussion of the spring equinox, the motif of the Descent Into the Underworld and the motif of the Dying and Rising God are closely related and have a lot of symbolic overlap. The difference is that a Descent usually involves a physical journey to the land of the dead, and the person taking this journey may not literally die to get there. In some stories, such as Inanna's Descent, a god or goddess journeys to the Underworld, dies there, and is then reborn, in a combination of both motifs.

While the Dying and Rising God is usually an agricultural deity, anyone can make the journey to the Underworld. Orpheus is a musician, Pwyll is a prince, and Izanagi is a creator deity.

Often, but not always, the person making the journey is following a recently deceased loved one, hoping to bring them back to the land of the living. These quests are almost always unsuccessful, reminding us that not even the gods can stop death. In other cases, the journey is to meet with an Underworld deity to ask for help or guidance, and these quests may actually succeed.

As you might have guessed, while the spring equinox is more focused on resurrection, the fall equinox is about making our peace with death. It is about acknowledging death as a natural part of the life cycle, one that all of us will experience someday. While we acknowledge the grief that death can bring, we also give thanks for death as the great bringer of peace, the end to all suffering, which breaks down old structures and ideas and composts them to nourish new life.

For queer witches, the fall equinox can be a powerful time to lay to rest the false selves we've had to live as to keep ourselves safe. For example, a trans witch might hold a funeral ritual for their deadname, or a pansexual witch might lay to rest their time in the closet. These are good deaths, because killing our false selves allows us to live more authentically.

Don't worry if you're not yet able to safely kill your false self. If you still have to stay closeted at work or around certain family members, this doesn't make you any less valid as a queer person. Always do whatever you need to do to keep yourself safe.

The fall equinox can also be a time to allow ourselves to grieve for relationships or communities we lost because of homophobia or transphobia. When I first came out as queer, I lost an entire religious community, including several close friends. I have relatives who still won't speak to me. And while I do think I'm better off without these people and their harmful beliefs in my life, I still mourn the connections that I lost because of hate. We can be glad a relationship is over and still feel grief about it ending.

If you have recently lost a relationship or had to leave a community because it wasn't safe and supportive for you as a queer person, the fall equinox can be a time to make space for that loss. Sit with yourself and allow yourself to feel your feelings, whatever they might be. There is no right or wrong way to grieve.

Sacred space for the fall equinox is decorated with fall leaves, seasonal fruits and vegetables (like apples and pumpkins), and anything else that represents autumn to you. You could also include symbols of death and the Underworld, such as images of skulls or pomegranates. The colors associated with this holiday are black, deep red, burnt orange, and dark green.

Samhain

Dates: November 1 in the Northern hemisphere, May 1 in the Southern hemisphere
Also Called: All Hallows' Eve
Theme: The Beloved Dead

Samhain (pronounced "SOW-en") is the final Gaelic festival of the year, and the last of the three harvest festivals. The origin of the word Samhain is unclear, but it may mean "summer's end."

In agrarian cultures, this was the time of year when the herds were brought in from the summer fields and culled. (Culling means reducing the size of a herd by slaughtering some of the animals, both to provide meat for humans and to make sure the remaining animals have enough food to get through the winter.) Historically, this was a three-day festival celebrated in Ireland, Scotland, and Wales.

Many of our modern Halloween celebrations have their roots in historical Samhain celebrations. Trick-or-treating, telling ghost stories, and wearing scary costumes are all traditions that can be traced back to Samhain celebrations, before All Hallows' Eve existed. Even carving jack 'o lanterns is an old Samhain tradition – before the introduction of pumpkins to Europe, they were made from turnips.

Of all the sabbats, Samhain is the one most closely associated with death and the dead. Although the Descent Into the Underworld is a focus of Fall Equinox celebrations, those stories usually involve the death of a god or hero who will be reborn in the spring. Samhain deals with human death, and with the dead themselves.

It is said that the veil between the world of the living and the world of the dead is thinnest at Samhain, allowing the dead to come back to visit their living loved ones. These visits from deceased loved ones are a source of comfort and joy to those who celebrate Samhain.

Historically, Samhain celebrations revolved around honoring our loved ones who have passed on into the land of the dead. In rural Ireland, families would set an extra place at the table for deceased loved ones and would leave the door to their home open or unlocked so that ghostly family members could stop in for a visit. England has a similar tradition called a *dumb supper*, in which an extra place is set for the dead and the entire meal is eaten in total silence. It was also common practice on Samhain to visit the graves of deceased family members and clean them up.

Modern witches often celebrate Samhain by setting up a ritual space for their ancestors. (Remember, ancestors can be your chosen family, not just blood relatives!) You may already have an ancestor shrine, but if you don't you might add images of your ancestors to your sacred space for this sabbat.

Celebrate your beloved dead by telling their stories and making offerings of the things they loved in life. If you have any family recipes that have been handed down for generations, cooking them and offering some to your ancestors makes a great Samhain ritual, even if the ancestors you honor are not related to you by blood.

If someone you love has died in the past year, Samhain would be an appropriate time to officially welcome them into your ancestor shrine. I always revamp my ancestor shrine on Samhain, adding new photos, candles, and personal items that belonged to my beloved dead. This includes adding a photo of anyone I know who has died since last Samhain and who I want to work with as an ancestor. I make offerings of tobacco, coffee, and one or more of my mama's family recipes. I also offer some of the Halloween candy we hand out to trick-or-treaters, because some of my ancestors are the people who took me trick-or-treating when I was a child.

Because Samhain is really about celebrating your own beloved dead, this can be a very personal and intimate holiday. At the same time, Samhain can be a time to express collective grief over losses in a community.

In the past, I have organized public Samhain rituals to honor those who lost their lives to police brutality and to the COVID-19 pandemic. These public rituals do the important job of holding space for shared grief, but they also make that grief visible and demand justice for those who have died. This can be a powerful way to mix spirituality with activism.

Sacred space for Samhain can include seasonal fruits and vegetables like pumpkins and squash, as well as those associated with death and the dead, like pomegranates or apples. You might include flowers, which are a common offering to the dead in many cultures, or modern Halloween symbols like jack-o-lanterns.

Gaelic Samhain celebrations historically included bonfires, so you might choose to make a fire outdoors or include candles in your indoor sacred space. Images of death, like skulls, bones, or mourning clothes, would also be appropriate. You should also include images of any specific ancestors you are honoring with your ritual. The colors associated with this holiday are black, white, deep red, orange, and gold.

Planning a Sabbat Ritual

As I've said before, there is no requirement to celebrate any of these holidays to be a witch, and there is no right or wrong way to celebrate any of the sabbats. I encourage you to do your own research into the parts of each sabbat that interest you. The parts of a holiday that are important for me may be different from the parts that are important for you.

This is why it is so important to craft your own rituals for each of the sabbats. Creating your own ritual allows you to really dig deep into the themes that matter to you.

When planning a ritual for one of the sabbats, think about what parts of the sabbat's lore and traditions resonate with you. If you are planning a May Day ritual, do you want to focus on the theme of sacred sex, the theme of fertility, or the Trickster archetype? If you are planning a Summer Solstice ritual, do you want to focus on divine opposites as a Sacred Marriage or as a pair of siblings? Choose the themes that feel most relevant to you right now.

Now, with those themes in mind, choose a focus for your ritual. This can be a specific goal, like manifesting a new job or moving on from a breakup, but it can also be more open. Your goal might simply be to connect with the rhythms of nature and the themes of this sabbat. Write your goal down, because this is the core of your ritual.

Once you have a clear goal, think about what ritual actions might be appropriate for this goal. If you're planning a May Day ritual with the goal of celebrating queer sexuality, your ritual action might be a sensual dance. If you're planning a Samhain ritual to honor those killed in transphobic hate crimes, you might read a list of victims' names while another witch sings a funeral chant. Choose a set of actions that make sense for your goal and the feelings you want your ritual to create.

As you plan out your ritual action(s), be realistic about what you can do with the people and resources available. A single witch practicing alone will not be able to pull off the kind of big, elaborate, public ritual that a group of witches could. A witch on a budget might need to keep finances in mind when choosing what to include in a ritual. Think about what is practical for your own situation.

Consider whether you want to base your ritual on a sacred story. If you are planning for the fall equinox, you might base your ritual on the story of Inanna's Descent. If you are planning for Yule, you might base your ritual on the story of the birth of Horus.

Think about how you want to incorporate this story into your ritual. Will you read or recite a version of the myth? Will you act the myth out, either by yourself or with other witches? Will you decorate your sacred space to reflect the story?

Now is also a good time to think about whether you want to call on any spiritual allies in your ritual. Do you want to invite local land spirits or your own ancestors to participate? Do you want to call on a deity? Not every ritual needs to have spirits involved, and some witches never call on spirits in their work, but it is something to consider. Just remember to always include an offering for any spirits you call on!

Once you have all these pieces together, write a plan for your ritual. This can be a loose outline or a detailed script. Your plan should cover every step from the opening of the ritual to its conclusion. Once you're done planning it out, read over it to make sure it flows well.

If you are planning a public or semi-public ritual, it's a good idea to practice at least once before performing the ritual in front of other people. This is especially important if your ritual involves multiple people. Practicing beforehand gives you a chance to work out any issues you might not have anticipated.

Accessibility Adjustment: Keep your own needs in mind as you write your rituals. If you know that you'll need to be sitting down for most of the ritual, plan to perform the ritual sitting down with your tools laid out within arm's reach. If you know that you're allergic to a plant that blooms outside this time of year, plan for an indoor ritual. The nice thing about writing your own rituals is being able to tailor them to your own needs.

Don't feel like you need to do an elaborate ritual for every sabbat. If all you can manage right now is to light a candle and say a few quick words while in bed, that is more than enough. And if you really don't feel well, it is absolutely okay to skip a sabbat. It doesn't make you any less of a witch.

Chapter 10

Queer Magic with Secular Holidays

Celebrating the Wheel of the Year can help us feel more connected to the cycle of the seasons and can be an opportunity to connect with other witches and pagans. However, many witches choose to incorporate other holidays into their personal practices, or may ignore the Wheel altogether.

The nice thing about making your own calendar of holidays is that you don't have to celebrate any holiday that doesn't resonate with you. If the Wheel of the Year, which is based on British agricultural seasons and Western European mythology, doesn't feel like a good fit for you, you don't need to include it in your practice.

Many witches choose to look to their own cultures for holidays to incorporate into their magic. For example, a Taiwanese witch may celebrate the Lunar New Year as the central holiday in their practice. Witches who practice a religion might also choose to incorporate religious holidays into their practice. Other witches choose to put their own magical spin on secular holidays. These secular celebrations will be the focus of this chapter.

The holidays included in this chapter are the ones I am most familiar with. Because I am an American witch living in the United States, these are mostly Western holidays. I understand that witches living in non-Western cultures may not celebrate Valentine's Day or Halloween, and that witches living in other Western countries might celebrate the same days differently. While I am limited by my own experiences, I hope this chapter will be a good example of how we can bring magic to secular celebrations, even if your culture has a very different set of major holidays.

I also want to address that some of the holidays included in this chapter, such as Valentine's Day and Halloween, were originally Christian religious celebrations. The last thing I want to do is disrespect the religious traditions associated with these holidays.

I have chosen to include these holidays here, even though they have religious origins, because modern celebrations of them (at least in the USA) are almost completely divorced from their religious roots. Because Christianity was tied to American national identity for a very long time, many of our national holidays have Christian themes that have been downplayed as our society became more religiously diverse.

In this chapter, I focus on the secular associations of these holidays. I think it is possible for us to be respectful of people who still find a religious meaning in these celebrations, while also enjoying our own festivities. Me enjoying my secular Halloween party does not take away from a Christian's heartfelt celebration of All Hallows' Eve. I believe there is room for both types of celebrations to coexist.

With that disclaimer out of the way, let's talk about ways to bring magic to a handful of popular holidays. As with Chapter 9, my hope is that this chapter will be a starting point for your own research, brainstorming, and ritual writing.

New Year's Day

Date: January 1
Theme: New Beginnings

New Year's Day is the beginning of the new calendar year in any culture that uses the Gregorian calendar. Because it is the beginning of the new year, this holiday is associated with new beginnings, fresh starts, and setting goals.

New Year's Day has many of the same associations as Yule. There is a feeling of excitement for the coming year. This is an excellent time for planning ahead and for dedicating yourself to the things you want to work on in the year to come.

Many people celebrate by staying up until midnight on New Year's Eve (December 31) so they can witness the moment one year ends and another begins. Some people choose to greet the new year at huge parties where they can celebrate with friends.

There are many, many superstitions around bringing in luck for the new year by wearing special clothes, eating special food, or doing a special action. I grew up in the Southeastern US, and I was taught that I should always clean my house on New Year's Eve because if the house is messy when the new year begins, I'll be bringing all of my "mess" (struggles and drama) into the new year with me. I was also taught that I should eat collard greens, black eyed peas, and cornbread on New Year's Day because these foods will bring in wealth in the new year. My partner and I still follow these superstitions every year.

You probably grew up with your own superstitious New Year's traditions. Why not use these traditions as a ritual to bless the new year?

New Year's Day is an appropriate time for any magic related to wishes, luck, or setting goals. This is a great opportunity for a fresh start, whatever that means for you right now. For queer witches, this can be a time to reflect on our identity and expression. Do you still feel comfortable with the label(s) you've been using for your gender and/or sexuality? Do you still feel like the way you dress and present yourself reflects who you are? Are you as involved with your local queer community as you would like to be?

Use New Year's Day to reflect on these questions and make a resolution to adjust anything that no longer feels quite right. Remember: identity is fluid, and you are allowed to change as you grow and learn.

Sacred space for New Year's Day should incorporate whatever colors and imagery you associate with this holiday.

In the USA, the colors most associated with New Year's Day are white and gold. You could load your New Year's altar up with lots of glitz and glamor to represent all the blessings and abundance you hope for in the coming year. Images associated with the passage of time, like clocks and calendars, would also be appropriate.

Valentine's Day

Date: February 14

Theme: Love

Valentine's Day is most commonly associated with romantic love, but it is really a day to celebrate loving connections of all kinds. Love between family members and friends is just as important as romantic or sexual love, and Valentine's Day reminds us of that. Some people have made this focus on platonic love explicit by celebrating "Galentine's Day," a celebration of friendship between women, alongside or instead of the traditional Valentine's Day. People of all genders can use this holiday to celebrate the people they love, whether friends, family, or lovers.

Witches in romantic or sexual relationships might use this holiday as a chance to remind our lovers how much we value them. Romantic relationships can be challenging, and it's never a bad idea to take a step back and simply be thankful for the person or people we've chosen as our partner(s). This can be a chance to reaffirm our commitment to our partners, celebrate the little wins in our relationships, and do something special for the ones we love.

For queer witches, especially witches in same-sex relationships, Valentine's Day is a time to celebrate our freedom to openly love who we love. We can sometimes take for granted that, at least in many places, it is relatively safe for us to go on public dates with our partners. Even if some people give us dirty looks or make rude comments, most of us are not in any physical danger when we are with our partners in public. In more progressive areas, we may not even get the dirty looks. This was not the case until very, very recently. Whether you are currently in a same-sex relationship or not, Valentine's Day is a day to thank our queer, activist ancestors and living elders for the work they did to make the world safer for us.

Sadly, this also means acknowledging that not every queer person has this privilege. In places such as the US state of Florida, which passed a notorious "Don't Say Gay" bill in 2022, many queer people live in fear of losing their jobs if they are open about their identity, especially if they work in Florida public schools. Even though a 2024 settlement gave some protections back to queer Florida teachers and students, many people in Florida and around the world still live in fear of being punished for their identity.

Valentine's Day can be a time to combine magic with activism to work for a world where no one has to hide their gender or sexuality for fear of losing their job, housing, or other essential needs.

For aromantic witches, Valentine's Day can be a time to reaffirm that romance is not a requirement for a happy life. For an aromantic Valentine's Day celebration, treat yourself with chocolate, flowers, or another little gift as a sign of self-love and independence. Celebrate with friends and chosen family. Give thanks for the loving, platonic relationships in your life. If you are in a queerplatonic relationship (a committed partnership between two or more people who are not romantically or sexually involved), you can celebrate your queerplatonic partner and reaffirm your commitment to them.

This is an appropriate time for any magic related to bringing love into your life, from self-love to friendship to a new romantic connection.

Here's a true story from my life: Several years ago, I did a spell to attract a new romantic relationship in the days leading up to Valentine's Day. The very next day, I was asked for a date by the person I would eventually marry! While I don't think that spell is the only reason our relationship has been successful, I'm sure it didn't hurt.

Sacred space for Valentine's Day should invoke the feeling of love. Colors associated with this holiday are pink and red. Images associated with love, like hearts, cupids, and red roses, are also strongly associated with this day. You can even use store-bought Valentine cards as part of your ritual!

April Fool's Day

Date: April 1
Theme: The Trickster/lighthearted mischief

April Fool's Day is traditionally a day for pranks, hoaxes, and other good-humored tricks. This mischievous energy is connected to the Trickster archetype. As we discussed in Chapter 9, the Trickster is all about challenging the dominant social order and causing change when it is needed. This is an archetype that resonates with many queer people, and it is easy to see why.

April Fool's Day can, of course, be a time to play jokes and pranks on our loved ones. Just make sure your jokes never cross the line from harmless fun into being mean. Scaring someone, causing them panic, or risking injury to them is cruel, not funny.

This can also be a time to sit with the Trickster energy and reflect on where in our life we need to challenge the status quo. Have you gotten comfortable with unhealthy patterns because accepting them is easier than working for change? Now is the time to address these issues, as long as it is physically safe to do so.

For queer folks, April Fool's Day can be a time to intentionally subvert gender and sexuality norms. If it is safe for you, try experimenting with different gendered clothing, hair, and makeup in public. If you have a partner who is willing, consider switching up your roles in the bedroom. Subversion is the theme of this holiday.

April Fool's Day is a good time for any magic related to creating change and shaking things up. This is an excellent time for magical activism and for any spell that deals with changing the way things have always been.

Sacred space for April Fool's Day should be fun, whimsical, and maybe a little mischievous. There are no colors associated with this holiday in pop culture, but you could use green because of its association with the Trickster archetype. Because of the theme of challenging the norm, you might even try decorating your space with colors you normally don't like. Images associated with this holiday could include animals associated with the Trickster, like foxes, rabbits, or spiders, as well as any image you associate with lighthearted fun. This holiday doesn't have a defined aesthetic the way New Year's Day and Valentine's Day do, so feel free to use your imagination!

Anniversary of the Stonewall Riots

Dates: June 28

Theme: Queer joy and triumph

Ever wondered why LGBTQ+ Pride is celebrated in June? It's because June 28 is the anniversary of the Stonewall riots, which sparked the beginning of a gay rights movement that would lead to many of the civil rights victories queer people enjoy today.

On June 28, 1969, police raided the Stonewall Inn in Greenwich Village, New York. The Stonewall Inn was a gay bar that provided a safe space for gay men, lesbians, drag queens, and transgender people at a time when homosexuality and crossdressing were illegal in the United States. On June 28, the patrons of the bar fought back and rioted against police brutality, alongside some of their neighbors. The riots were followed by protesting, and the people involved organized to eventually form the gay liberation movement.

The first gay pride parades were held on the first anniversary of the Stonewall riot. The rest is, quite literally, history.

The Anniversary of Stonewall is a time to celebrate how far the queer community has come. It is a time to celebrate queer joy. It is a time to be in community with other queer people. The vibe of this holiday is happy, triumphant, and supportive, just like many modern Pride parades.

This is also a time to give thanks for the queer ancestors and elders who fought tooth and nail for the rights we enjoy today. We can honor our ancestors by giving offerings and by telling their stories. We can honor queer elders by lifting them up, thanking them for their work, and working to make strong connections across generations.

We should never forget that it took years of organizing and activism to win the most basic rights for our community. These were frightening times, and peaceful protest was not always an option. The Anniversary of Stonewall is a good time to reflect on the relationship between peaceful protest, violent revolution, and political change.

This is an appropriate time for any magic related to your queer identity and community, and for any magic related to social or political change. Sacred space for this holiday should be beautiful. Colors associated with this holiday are the rainbow, of course, but also lavender and pink, both colors that have historically been associated with gay men and lesbians. Consider including photos from the Stonewall riots and/or images of queer ancestors you feel especially close to. You can also include silk or paper flowers, which were a favorite of many of the drag queens who frequented the Stonewall Inn.

Halloween

Date: October 31
Theme: death, the spirit world, inner child

Halloween may be related to Samhain (see Chapter 9), but it really has become its own thing in modern popular culture. Halloween still has some associations with death and the dead, but secular Halloween traditions tend to focus much more on ghost stories, flirting with the supernatural, and mischievous fun.

If you don't want to dig into the history of Samhain and All Hallows' Eve, you can draw from modern Halloween traditions instead. Take inspiration from trick-or-treaters, scary movies, and pumpkin-flavored everything. Lean into the spooky fun of modern Halloween celebrations.

This is a great time of year to flirt with the things that scare us. Maybe you've been putting off doing something because it intimidates you. Maybe there's something you've always wanted to do, but you've always chickened out. Use the energy of Halloween to take the plunge and do the thing.

We can also enjoy more lighthearted fun at this time of year. Ghost stories, scary movies, and haunted house attractions can all be fun ways to get our hearts racing without getting too deep. Not all the work we do as witches needs to be super serious!

I also see Halloween as a time to connect with my inner child, probably because it is such a kid-oriented holiday. As we get older, we sometimes become disconnected from our childlike sense of wonder, whimsy, and joy. It can be deeply healing to let ourselves feel like kids again.

If you want to connect with your inner child, Halloween is a great time to do it. Consider dressing up for the holiday, even if no one else is going to see you. Carve a jack 'o lantern. Buy yourself a bucket of Halloween candy or bake some of your own sweet treats. Rewatch that horror movie you saw for the first time when you were way too young. Let your kid self run wild, just for one night.

Of course, if you have children of your own or are involved with a loved one's children, trick-or-treating together can be as fun for you as it is for them. Even if there are no kids in your life, you can still participate by answering the door and handing out candy to the neighborhood trick-or-treaters.

Halloween has a deep connection to mischief and subversion, which makes it a very queer holiday. For example, Halloween costumes can be a low stakes way to play around with gender and sexuality.

One of my favorite queer traditions is going to midnight showings of *The Rocky Horror Picture Show* on Halloween night. This cult classic movie is incredibly queer in a fun, weird, campy way, and I absolutely recommend it if you haven't experienced it. Showings of this film have many traditions and rituals involving props, audience participation, and a "shadow cast" acting the film out on stage as it plays. It's an incredibly queer-affirming space and is something I think everyone should experience at least once.

Halloween is an appropriate time for any work related to spirits or the spirit world. (Just remember the etiquette we discussed earlier in this book.) It is also a good time for magic related to overcoming fears or connecting to your inner child.

Sacred space for Halloween can be as warm and cozy or as spooky and scary as you make it. Colors associated with this holiday are orange, black, red, and purple. Images and symbols associated with this holiday are pumpkins and jack 'o lanterns, skulls, spiders and spiderwebs, tombstones, and anything else creepy and macabre. Feel free to use commercial Halloween decorations on your altar!

Other Holidays

Queer witches might also choose to hold rituals on days that are important to the queer community or to a subset of the community. You might choose to ritually celebrate any of the following days:

- February 20-26: Aromantic Spectrum Awareness Week
- March 31: International Transgender Day of Visibility
- April 6: International Asexuality Day
- Third Friday of April: Day of Silence
- April 18: Nonbinary Parents Day
- April 26: Lesbian Visibility Day
- May 17: International Day Against Homophobia, Transphobia, and Biphobia
- May 24: Pansexual and Panromantic Awareness and Visibility Day
- June: Pride Month
- June 1: LGBTQ Families Day
- June 12: Pulse Remembrance
- June 26: Anniversary of the United States Supreme Court making marriage equality federal law
- July 14: International Nonbinary People's Day
- July 16: International Drag Day
- September 23: Celebrate Bisexuality Day
- October: LGBTQ+ History Month
- October 8: International Lesbian Day
- October 11: National Coming Out Day
- Last Full Week of October: Asexual Awareness Week
- First Sunday of November: Transgender Parent Day
- November 13-19: Transgender Awareness Week
- November 20: Transgender Day of Remembrance
- December 8: Pansexual/Panromantic Pride Day

These holidays can be a chance to celebrate your identity, connect with queer ancestors, and work your queer magic. For help planning your rituals, look back at the "Planning a Sabbat Ritual" section from Chapter 9.

Conclusion

As we reach the end of our journey together, I hope this book has given you new tools to craft your own queer-affirming magical practice. I hope you feel empowered to step onto a path that not only accommodates your identity, but uplifts and celebrates it.

Witchcraft and queer identity have always danced close together in the margins and liminal spaces outside of mainstream spirituality. When we step into this lineage of queer magic, we see our identities reflected in the sacred elements, in the tapestry of the stars and planets, and in the web of plant and animal life. We can call on our ancestors for comfort and for power. We can bask in the divine love of gods, goddesses, and holy ones whose gender and sexuality are not so different from our own.

Whether we choose to join the dance as solo practitioners or as part of a community, we can create safe, affirming spaces not just for our own people, but for all marginalized folks. May our example empower others to bring their full, authentic selves to their spiritual practice.

This book is the beginning of your journey along the path of queer witchcraft, not the end. Remember, we are all individuals, and each of us will connect with these sacred mysteries in our own unique way. Now that you've seen one queer witch's approach, think about where you might do things differently. I have shown you one possible path, but I encourage you to do your own wayfinding and pathmaking as you continue in your practice.

If you came to this book as an ally, I thank you for taking steps to be a better friend and support person to the queer witches in your life. I hope I have helped you to craft a practice that is not only more welcoming to the LGBTQ+ community, but more affirming of your own identity as well.

Remember that you are sacred, divine, and magical, no matter who you are or how you identify. Your gender and your love are holy. The magic you make has the potential to heal yourself, your community, and the world. I know you will do incredible things, and I am grateful to have been part of your journey.

I leave you with many blessings and much love.

About the Author

Hailing from the foothills of the Appalachian mountains, Sam Wise (she/they) is a Reclaiming witch and eclectic pagan with years of experience combining magic, activism, and queer culture. Sam is a member of AIRA (the Ableism-Impacted Reclaiming Alliance), where they serve as the current representative to BIRCH (Reclaiming's decision-making body). They are also a member of the Fellowship of Fire and Ice, where they are part of the ritual team. Sam has a passion for combining folk traditions with modern practices to create accessible, affirming magic.

Outside the magic circle, Sam can usually be found behind a large pile of books in her Atlanta home. She enjoys tabletop games, Renaissance fairs, metal shows, black coffee, and snuggling with her many animal companions.

Sam is on Instagram and Tumblr at @samwisethewitch and on TikTok at @authorsamwise. She also posts articles and updates on her website, samwisethewitch.com. She can be reached via email at samwiseauthor@gmail.com.

Appendix

Queer Magic in Community

It's entirely possible to have a fulfilling magical practice without ever interacting with another witch. You may enjoy working on your own, and there isn't anything wrong with that. On the other hand, many of us enjoy sharing space with other witches. This chapter focuses on how to find a queer-affirming group – or start your own!

Finding a Group

Before starting your own coven or group, I recommend looking at your options for joining an existing group. Joining an established group will mean less work for you, and the group may have access to resources you wouldn't have access to on your own.

When looking for a group to join, it's helpful to think about the type of group you'd like to be part of. Most groups focused on witchcraft fall into one of two categories:

- *General or open groups* are focused on witchcraft more generally and are usually open to witches from all walks of life. In these groups, witches from many different practices come together in solidarity.
- *Tradition-specific groups* are dedicated to a single witchcraft tradition, such as Wicca, Feri, Traditional Witchcraft, or some other path. Members of these groups focus on supporting each other in their chosen tradition.

Neither of these types of group is better or worse than the other, but they cater to different approaches to magic. If you prefer secular witchcraft, or if your personal practice is very eclectic (meaning it draws from many different sources), you might prefer a general group. Even if you follow a specific tradition, a general group can still help you to see how other people do things and to learn about other approaches to magic. If you are dedicated to a witchcraft tradition or are considering joining a tradition, joining a group dedicated to that path can be helpful.

Depending on your interests, you may also consider looking into other spiritual groups that aren't focused on witchcraft. For example, if you are interested in working with the Hellenic gods, you might consider joining a Hellenic pagan group so you can connect to other worshipers. The guidelines given in this chapter for finding a queer-affirming group can apply to these other groups as well as to more witchcraft-focused ones.

Now that you know what type of group you want to join, start thinking about what kind of group structure you are interested in. Here are some common group structures to consider:

- *Social groups* are mainly focused on being a space for witches to get together, hang out, and talk about magic and life. These groups may offer classes or hold rituals, but the main goal of the group is to provide a safe social space for its members. They may offer events like coffee and conversation brunches, movie nights, or coven socials.
- *Teaching groups* are mainly focused on teaching students. These groups are usually run by a teacher or group of teachers and will usually offer regular classes on witchcraft and magic. These groups may hold rituals or offer social spaces, but the main goal of the group is to pass on knowledge and skills to students.
- *Ritual groups* are mainly focused on coming together for spells and other rituals. For example, a group may come together for rituals on each of the sabbats on the Wheel of the Year. These groups may teach classes or offer social spaces, but the main goal of the group is to hold group rituals.

- *Study groups* are somewhere between social groups and teaching groups. Study groups are mainly focused on being a space for witches to come together and discuss their studies into witchy topics. Instead of offering classes, study groups are more like book clubs, with a group of students working through the same material together. Study groups may be facilitated by a teacher, or they may be a group of new students supporting each other's quests for knowledge.

Some groups combine more than one of these structures. Some covens teach classes, host social gatherings, and hold public rituals. Other groups limit their focus to a single goal.

Think about what your goals are for joining a group. Are you looking for a teacher to help you learn new skills? Are you looking for people to join in ritual? Are you looking for witchy friends? Choose the group structure that best supports your goals.

Once you know what you are looking for, it's time to start seeking out a group. You can look for groups in-person or online – just know that both in-person groups and online groups have pros and cons.

In-person groups give you face-to-face time with other witches, but you may have to travel long distances for group meetings, depending on where you live and where the group is. Online groups have more flexibility and allow people to participate from anywhere, but they may have to deal with conflicting time zones or with people "ghosting" (disappearing without an explanation) when they lose interest in the group. Only you know what will be the best fit for you.

If you are looking for an in-person group, it's best to focus your search on your local area. If at all possible, go out and talk to people in person. Many groups don't have a social media presence and only advertise by word of mouth, so you may need to ask around to get information about how to join.

Good places to start looking for an in-person witchcraft group include:

- Metaphysical stores, botanicas, occult bookstores, and other businesses that cater to witchy types.
- Pagan Pride festivals.
- Interfaith councils.
- Unitarian Universalist churches. (Unitarian Universalists believe that each person's spiritual journey is different and unique, and they are open to many approaches to spirituality. Most UU churches have some witches and pagans among their members. As a bonus, most UU groups are queer-affirming.)
- Student groups at colleges or universities. (Most large universities will have a pagan student union, and these groups may be able to recommend resources even if you aren't a student at their school.)
- Renaissance festivals, medieval fairs, and historic reenactment events. (Seriously, you'd be surprised how many witches hang out at these events – just be cautious, as some history-based events can also attract people with very conservative beliefs.)

These are only a few of the places you might go to find information about local groups. There may be other people and places in your community that can point you in the right direction.

You can also check social media for groups in your area. Facebook is a good place to look for groups in a specific location. You can also check Reddit, especially if your city has its own subreddit. It's also worth checking other social media like Instagram, Tik Tok, and Tumblr, although it may be harder to find what you're looking for on these sites. Some groups will also use event-planning sites like Eventbrite, Meetup, or a local event board.

If you are posting on a public forum asking for information, be wary of trolls. It's always a good idea to post anonymously if possible, and to avoid giving your real name or any other identifying information. Follow basic internet safety guidelines like checking people's profiles to make sure they are who they say they are, fact-checking any information they give you, and never giving out your address or phone number.

If you are looking for an online group, most of your search will probably happen online. You can absolutely start by doing a Google search, or using a different search engine to look for groups that match your interests. Just be aware that this isn't always the most efficient way to find groups. Your search may turn up false pings (web pages that aren't actually relevant to your search), old or outdated information, and other junk. Don't be discouraged if your search doesn't immediately bring up results. Just because they aren't showing up on Google doesn't mean they aren't out there.

When looking for an online group, social media can be a great resource. Since your search isn't limited to a single location, you'll probably have better luck on Instagram, TikTok, and Tumblr than if you were looking for a local group. Facebook can also be a good place to look for online groups.

If you are interested in a specific witchcraft tradition, you can head to Reddit to look for groups. This is especially useful if the tradition you are interested in has its own subreddit.

You can also look to witches you admire to see if they recommend any online groups. You might look your favorite witchy author up on social media and see if they have a Discord server, Facebook group, or similar social group. I have found several excellent groups this way.

In my experience, finding a group is the hard part. But just because a group is out there doesn't mean it's the right group for you. The next step is to decide whether you want to join up.

Joining a Group

Before you ever attend a group meeting, find out what that group believes and what rules they have in place. You can often find this information on the group's website and/or social media pages. If the group doesn't have social media, ask if they have an information pamphlet for new members or if you can speak with one of the group's leaders about their beliefs and rules.

Safe groups are transparent about what they believe, what (if any) tradition they are part of, who is in charge, what the group's rules are, and how those rules are enforced. This information should be readily available to people who are interested in the group.

Be very, very wary of any group that hides this information or insists that only members can know what they do. While it's reasonable to want to protect the group's privacy, this level of secrecy is deeply suspicious. Ask yourself why they feel the need to hide what they are doing from other witches.

Groups that are very secretive about who they are and what they believe may be hiding a connection to dangerous groups such as white supremacists, trans-exclusive radical feminists (TERFs), or other hate groups. They may be using their group as a way to radicalize people by slowly pulling them into a hate movement. While not all groups that are overly secretive are hiding a connection to a hate group, it's best to avoid any group that isn't transparent with basic information, just to be safe.

One thing to look for in a group is a clear *non-discrimination statement*. A non-discrimination statement is exactly what it sounds like – a statement that the group will not exclude anyone based on features like race, ethnicity, gender, sexuality, or ability. This is the most important sign of whether or not a group is safe for LGBTQ+ witches.

A good non-discrimination statement is more than a simple "All are welcome" message. It should explicitly name the different aspects of identity that the group is aware of (race, gender, sexuality, etc.) and should explain what the group is doing to make marginalized people feel safe and included. It should clearly state that hate and bullying are not tolerated and should explain how the group will deal with hate if it occurs.

I recommend avoiding any group that doesn't have a strong non-discrimination statement. At best, a lack of a non-discrimination statement shows that a group isn't prepared to have hard conversations about identity and is not committed to protecting its members. At worst, a group without a non-discrimination statement may actively exclude people based on race, gender, sexuality, or other identity markers, or may even have ties to hate movements.

Another red flag is what I like to call a *false non-discrimination statement*. This is a statement that looks like it's saying the group is inclusive at first glance, but is actually laying the groundwork for protecting bigots. These statements usually say that the group doesn't discriminate based on political beliefs, but they don't mention race, gender, sexuality, or any other identity marker. What this is really saying is that the group welcomes people with harmful or hateful beliefs and that group leadership will not stop these people from "sharing their beliefs" by harassing other group members. If a group has a false non-discrimination statement, I recommend avoiding that group.

Some groups have blanket "no politics" rules, which is less of a red flag and more of a yellow light – as in, slow down and be cautious.

The idea that it is possible to "stay out of politics" comes from a place of privilege. People who have these beliefs usually have *normative identities,* which means they hold one or more identities that our society treats as the default or even as superior. For example, white, straight, cisgender, and able-bodied are all normative identities. To put a complex issue very simply, the more normative identities someone holds, the more social privilege they have.

Think of it like right-handedness vs. left-handedness. The world is built for right-handed people. Many schools use right-handed desks. Most scissors are made to be used with the right hand. In English, we write from left to right, which means a left-handed person has to drag their hand across the page, which can smear some types of ink.

Right-handed people usually don't notice these things, because they aren't being negatively impacted by them. They don't experience the frustration of sitting awkwardly in a desk that isn't built for them or trying to cut paper with scissors that don't work properly in their hands. Right-handed people might never think about these frustrations, but for left-handed people they are a daily reality. You can see how the same might be true when it comes to race, gender, disability, and more.

It is easy for someone with normative identities to stay out of politics because politics do not have a big impact on their daily life. To them, talking about politics is something uncomfortable that can be avoided to keep the peace. It isn't a matter of survival like it is for many marginalized people.

The problem with groups that have a "no politics" rule is that simply existing as a queer person is a political act, whether we intend it that way or not. In a country that has homophobic and transphobic laws on the books, being openly gay or trans has real political consequences. And because so much of Western politics is centered on an "us vs. them" mindset, simply being ourselves as queer people can be seen (incorrectly) as an attack on more conservative political beliefs.

"No politics" rules become a problem when they are used to silence queer people (and other marginalized groups) and to police how we express ourselves. Queer people are essentially forced back into the closet to protect the group's peace. While this may not be as openly hateful as refusing to allow queer members, it can be just as harmful, if not more so.

For all of these reasons, I recommend avoiding groups with blanket rules against politics in group spaces.

One last note on discrimination: many groups are adults-only, and that on its own isn't necessarily a red flag. A group may have an adults-only rule because some of their events have sexual elements, which may or may not be something you're comfortable with. But many groups have this rule simply because they don't want to risk getting into trouble with angry parents who don't want their teenager dabbling in witchcraft. Requiring all group members to be legal adults gets around the need to get consent from parents for minors to participate. This is the same reason many queer events are adults-only.

If a group has an adults-only rule but also has a good non-discrimination statement, that group is probably still safe. You can always ask why they felt the need to limit the group to adults.

If you have looked into the group's beliefs and practices and still think they might be a good fit for you, and the group has a good non-discrimination statement, ask if you can attend an event as a guest. Not all groups allow this, but if it is allowed it's a great way to get a feel for whether the group is what you're looking for.

If you can't attend the group as a guest, ask if you could meet a few members of the group to talk about their experiences. Ideally, you would talk to at least one person in leadership and at least one person who isn't in leadership. Ask them to meet you in a public place, like a library, park, or coffee shop, so you can ask them a few questions.

Be wary of groups that require you to give them money before you are allowed to participate. While it's normal to charge a small fee for classes or to ask people to help pay for ritual supplies, it isn't normal to expect someone to pay a membership fee for a group they aren't committed to yet. This is especially true if the membership fee is very expensive, or if group leadership refuses to explain why the fee is required. You could be dealing with a scam.

If possible, attend a few group events before you decide whether or not to join. If this isn't possible, ask if the group offers trial memberships or another way for you to try the group out before making a big commitment.

There's no need to commit to a group immediately. Take some time to get to know the people in the group, get a feel for their rituals, and find out where you fit into the group dynamic. Think of it like dating. You probably want to go on several dates with someone before deciding whether to commit to a relationship with them. In the same way, you should take time to get to know a group before deciding whether to join. You may even want to "date around" and try several groups before choosing one or two to join.

Starting Your Own Group

You may not be able to find an existing group that meets your needs. Maybe you really want to be part of an in-person community, but there are no queer-affirming groups that meet in-person in your area. Maybe you work nights and weekends and can't find a group that works for your schedule. Maybe you want to join a group dedicated to a specific deity or pantheon. In these cases, you may want to start your own group.

If you choose to start your own group, be prepared to do a lot of work. As the founder of the group, you'll need to handle advertising, vetting new members, writing by-laws and statements of belief, assigning leadership roles, addressing accessibility concerns, and more. Check in with yourself and make sure you have the time and energy for a project like this before you dive in.

When starting your own group, the first step is to choose a group focus. Will your group be open or tradition-specific? Will it be a social group, a teaching group, a ritual group, a study group, or a combination of multiple group structures? Will you have a special focus, like dedicating the group to a specific deity or focusing only one kind of magic? What are your goals for this new group?

My advice is to choose a narrow focus when just starting out so you don't spread your resources too thin. Instead of trying to be everything to everyone, choose one thing and focus on doing that one thing well. When the group has been going for a while and everything is running smoothly, you can expand to other areas.

Keep in mind that open groups will be easier to find members for, simply because they have a broader focus. It's easier to find people interested in witchcraft in general than to find people interested in a specific tradition or path.

This doesn't mean you can't start a tradition-specific group, but just know it may take longer to find members than it would for an open group. You'll probably need to put a lot of time and energy into advertising, at least at first.

If your group is dedicated to a specific magical tradition, consider either offering classes on your tradition or referring people who are interested to a trusted teacher within the tradition. Many people may be interested but won't have experience in your tradition. Helping them in their study will help them know if your group is a good fit for them and will help your tradition grow.

Once you've chosen a focus for your group, you'll need to decide whether your group will be open to the public. Your group might be completely open to the public, or it may be private or semi-private. There are pros and cons to all of these approaches.

Public groups are groups that hold classes or rituals in public places such as parks and libraries. These groups usually welcome any interested member of the public to join them, at least as an observer. Because public groups require so much more management and logistics, groups that are truly 100% open to the public are rare.

A public group may be the best option if you plan to focus on activist work. If you are hosting a protest, you want to have as many people standing and marching with you as possible. Because peaceful activism already requires a lot of logistical support and coordination with local government, a group that organizes frequent protests and community service projects is more likely to have the infrastructure in place to support a public group.

Some teaching groups are also open to the public. These groups hold free or low-cost classes or other educational events in public places, which allows them to reach any member of the public who might be interested.

The biggest downside to running a public group is that these groups receive the most attention from people outside the group, which leaves them vulnerable to harassment and troll behavior. For example, a group that holds public sabbat rituals in a local park may attract backlash from local anti-witchcraft or anti-pagan groups. This could be individuals yelling rude comments or attempting to interrupt the ritual, or it could be a full blown protest with picketing and marching. Groups with public-facing social media pages are also vulnerable to online harassment. For these reasons, public groups need to have a very solid plan in place for peacefully dealing with this harassment.

Another downside to running a public group is that public groups require much more intense management. You may need permits to hold events in public spaces, and more people at your events means more logistics to manage. For large public rituals, your group will be responsible for providing water, food, shelter, bathroom facilities, and emergency first aid, potentially for a large number of people. Your group's leadership will also have to be prepared to work with the public, including managing the group's public image in your community. Running a public group is a lot of work, and it's more than one person can realistically do on their own.

Private groups are closed to the general public and hold private meetings for group members only. These groups are usually smaller, and they usually have a process in place for vetting people who are interested in joining. Some private groups do not accept new members at all. Sometimes, these are groups of friends who decide to come together to share their practice. Because of this, some private groups are very casual.

The biggest benefit to a private group is, of course, privacy. These groups usually meet in a member's home or in a private venue, which gives them more separation from the general public. The group may not have social media, or may have social media groups that are only visible to members. Because of this, private groups are much less likely to face harassment or trolling compared to public groups. This can be wonderful for creating safe spaces for queer witches and other marginalized magical folks.

The biggest downside to a private group is that they can easily become cliques. If your goal in starting a group is to meet new witchy friends, a group that is 100% private will make it harder to do that. In a small group that does not accept new members, it can be easy to fall into clique roles – one or two members become the leaders (even if they aren't actually in leadership) and the other members become their followers. Small, private groups also have a tendency to become repetitive, always performing the same rituals or revisiting the same discussion topics over and over again.

Semi-private groups are open to the public in some ways, but some of the group's activity is for members only. For example, a semi-private group may have a "members and guests only" rule for rituals, but have public-facing social media pages and teach classes that are open to anyone interested. In my experience, this is the most common approach to working with the public, especially for smaller groups.

Semi-private groups are able to protect the privacy of their members while also being involved in the community around them. These groups are also able to educate the community about witchcraft while also creating private, sacred space for important rituals. It can really be the best of both worlds.

One downside to semi-private groups is that members may disagree on how open the group should be to the public. Some members might believe that rituals should be for members only, while others might believe rituals should be open to visitors who are interested in joining but want to try it out first. Some members might want to host public rituals once or twice a year, and others might feel that all rituals should be private. Members may also disagree on how much should be shared on public-facing social media pages.

To deal with these conflicts, semi-private groups need a solid decision-making system that makes sure that everyone feels heard and that decisions are made as a group. It's also a good idea for public-facing roles (like managing social media or speaking at interfaith events) to be given to group members who are more comfortable working with the public.

Think about what you want to do with your group, then ask yourself how public or private the group needs to be to accomplish those goals. If you are founding a group with other witches, make sure you are all in agreement on how much privacy the group will have.

I want to note that privacy is not the same thing as secrecy. A group can be private and still be transparent about their beliefs and about what they do when asked. A group being private is not an excuse to keep secrets.

Once you've decided on the basic structure and focus of your group and on how public or private it will be, it's time to establish a decision making process. It's best to have this process in place before making any more decisions, so that future decisions can be made in a way the group agrees is fair.

The best decision making processes are democratic and allow every member of the group to have their voice heard, even if they disagree with the majority. I recommend avoiding *autocratic decision making,* which puts all of the power in the hands of a single decision maker like a president or a high priestex. (*Priestex* is a gender-neutral alternative to priest or priestess.) This allows a single person to make decisions for the whole group without listening to how group members feel on the issue. It also creates opportunities for the group leader to abuse their power, or for the group to become unofficially dedicated to building up the leader's ego. It's best to keep this kind of power imbalance out of our spiritual spaces.

I also recommend avoiding an *oligarchy,* where decisions for the group are made by a small group of leaders. At first glance, this may seem more democratic than autocratic decision making because power is spread out between several people, but a small council or steering committee can become just as oppressive as an autocratic leader. Oligarchies can lead to a small group taking over all decision-making without listening to what the majority of the group has to say. It can also turn groups into cliques where everything is decided by the ruling committee, and creates opportunities for abuses of power.

One option for truly democratic decision making is to make decisions by voting. In this decision making process, every issue is put forward to the group. Then, group members are given an opportunity to suggest solutions. All of the suggestions should be written down. Once everyone who has a suggestion has been allowed to speak, each group member can vote for the solution they think is best. The votes are counted, and the solution with the most votes is the one the group will choose.

Voting is a familiar process to those of us who live in modern democratic countries like the United States, the United Kingdom, and the nations of the European Union. Because the process is familiar, it's usually easy for group members to get behind voting on issues. Voting is also a quick and efficient way to make sure every member of the group is involved in making a decision.

We don't always have time to call a meeting to vote on issues. Sometimes, the group needs to respond quickly. When this happens, the group can use *asynchronous voting* to make the decision.

In an asynchronous voting process, group leadership can create a group text message, an email list, or a social media thread visible only to group members. This channel should be open for at least 24 hours. Members can use the channel to suggest solutions, just like they would at a formal meeting. Once all the suggestions have been heard, group leadership can make a poll or survey and send it out to members of the group. Group members can use this poll to vote for a solution. At the end of the 24 hours (or other agreed-upon time frame), the solution with the most votes is the one the group will move forward with. This process should be used only for emergency decisions.

The biggest downside to voting is that because it uses the majority vote to make a decision, some members of the group may be disappointed by the outcome. There will probably be members who vote for a solution that does not win, and they may not like or support the solution the majority chooses. This can lead to bitterness and hard feelings within the group.

The fairest way to make group decisions is through *consensus.* Consensus means the entire group comes together to discuss the issue and choose a single solution that everyone can support.

This is the most time consuming way to make decisions, but it is also the best way to make sure everyone is satisfied with the solution.

In consensus-based decision making, every choice must be *unanimous,* meaning the entire group is in agreement. This may mean it takes longer to achieve a solution, but it often leads to a stronger feeling of group unity and more buy-in from group members. When a group is truly in consensus, every member feels like they are part of the decision-making process, even if they are not 100% happy with the final decision.

Making decisions by consensus does not mean there are never disagreements. Instead, disagreements are discussed in a calm, rational way, with feedback from the entire group. Instead of voting for one of two options, the group looks for a compromise that both sides can be satisfied with, even if it isn't exactly what either side wanted.

Making decisions by consensus is less familiar than voting for most witches, but you may have experience with this kind of decision-making if you have been involved in activism or social reform work. Here is an example of what a consensus process might look like for a group of witches:

> When a decision needs to be made, the group gathers for a meeting to seek a solution. In-person meetings are preferable because they allow for the most natural communication, but video calls are a good alternative if meeting in person isn't possible. All group members should know in advance what issue is being discussed at the meeting. Anyone who can't make it to the meeting is encouraged to phone in or to write down their thoughts on the issue being discussed and choose another member to read their thoughts to the group.
>
> Before the meeting, one person is chosen to present the issue to the group. This person opens the meeting by

introducing the issue (for example, choosing a theme for an upcoming public ritual) and answers any questions the group may have. After the issue has been introduced, the floor is opened for anyone present to share a potential solution. Each suggestion is written down, preferably in a place where all group members can see it.

Every member of the group is given a chance to speak, even if they don't have a solution to suggest. Their opinions and insights are still a valuable part of the decision-making process. This can take a while, so leadership makes sure to give plenty of time for discussion and to schedule short breaks.

Once everyone has spoken, the person leading the meeting asks the group to discuss which solution they will choose. Sometimes, the group immediately agrees on one solution and the meeting ends quickly. More often, there will be some disagreement within the group that will need to be talked out. If needed, the group's leadership might remind everyone that the goal is to reach a compromise everyone can get behind, not to argue over which approach is best. When someone voices an objection or a concern, they are taken seriously and the group discusses how to address their concerns.

The meeting only ends when there are no more objections to the solution the group has chosen. Usually, this comes after several adjustments and compromises. Even though some group members may be disappointed because they would have preferred a different solution, they are comfortable with the decision reached by the group.

Like voting, the consensus process can be done asynchronously in emergencies when a decision must be made quickly. Group leadership can create a group text message, an email list, or a social media thread visible only to group members. This channel should be open for at least 24 hours. Members can use the channel to suggest solutions, just like they would at a formal meeting. Once all the suggestions have been heard, the group discusses solutions and works through disagreements via text, just like they would in person. When everyone agrees on a path forward, the channel can be closed.

Consensus is great for helping members of the group feel unified on important issues, and it is a great way to make sure everyone's voice is heard. Because all group members have a chance to make sure their concerns are addressed, there are fewer bitter feelings even when there are disagreements.

The biggest downside to consensus is that it takes much longer than other types of decision-making. The discussion process can sometimes stretch out over weeks or months if there is a lot of disagreement within the group. This means it tends to take longer to get new projects off the ground.

Groups that are very large may run into logistical issues with the consensus process. If a group has several hundred members, or has members spread out across multiple time zones, it can be difficult to get everyone together for a meeting and to make sure everyone's voice is heard.

The best way to deal with these logistical issues is to break the group down into *cells,* which are smaller decision-making groups. For example, a group spread out across the United States might have a West Coast cell, a Midwest cell, and an East Coast cell. Each cell has their own consensus process, then chooses a representative to take their findings to the larger group. The representatives of all the different cells come together for another consensus process, with each representative speaking for their cell.

Whether you choose to use voting or consensus to make decisions for your group, it is important to have a decision-making process in place before you choose leaders or start accepting new members.

Your group's first decision will be working together to write a *group agreement.* A group agreement is a short, written statement that gives people a basic idea of what your group believes, what values you stand for, and what norms members are expected to follow. Group agreements are an important way for us to make it clear from the beginning that our group is a safe space for all queer identities and that homophobia, transphobia, and other types of hate will not be tolerated.

Your group agreement may be just one paragraph or may take up a whole page. It's best to avoid making it too long, because you want people to be able to read it quickly.

Here is an example of a group agreement:

> Our group is a place for queer witches from different paths to come together and to share in magic and fellowship. We embrace the label of witch as a symbol of resistance to heteronormative and patriarchal spirituality. We embrace the word queer as an inclusive label for all people who do not fit into a cisgender, heterosexual mold. We believe that the Earth is sacred, that each person contains within them the spark of the divine, and that the human body is holy.
>
> We welcome queer witches and their allies from all walks of life, including all races, all genders, all gender presentations, all sexualities, all levels of ability, and all economic and cultural backgrounds. We do not exclude anyone for the gods and holy ones they choose to work with. We strive to be an antiracist community and to create safe, protective spaces for BIPOC witches. We strive to keep all events and rituals accessible for the diverse bodies within our community.

> This group is a place for witches to support and uplift each other and to celebrate the diversity of our magical paths. We strive to keep this community respectful and uplifting. We have a zero tolerance policy for harassment and bullying of any kind. White supremacy, racism, homophobia, transphobia, misogyny, ableism, and other hateful ideologies are not compatible with our values and are not tolerated in our space.

Of course, you don't have to use this example group agreement. (Although you are welcome to if you feel it fits your group!) I share this example not because this is what you have to use, but as an example to get you thinking and a jumping off point for writing your own group agreement.

Your group agreement should answer the following questions:

- What is the purpose/goal of your group?
- Why call yourself witches? What does "witch" mean for your group?
- Is your group dedicated to a specific spiritual tradition, or open to anyone?
- What, if any, are some beliefs that are shared by all your members?

Your group agreement should also include a non-discrimination statement, as discussed earlier in this appendix. Remember, a good non-discrimination statement makes it clear that your group is aware of the issues facing marginalized folks and is taking steps to create a safe, affirming, and protective space for people with different identities.

Once you've written a group agreement, it should be approved by the group, either by vote or by consensus. It is very important that all founding group members are satisfied with the group agreement before moving forward.

Growing Your Group

Once you've chosen a focus for your group, decided how public vs. private it will be, chosen a decision-making process, and created a group agreement, you are almost ready to start holding events and accepting new members. But first, you'll need to assign group roles.

Group roles include jobs like priestexes and teachers, but also less glamorous jobs like treasurer, secretary, and publicist. Yes, you need someone to lead rituals and/or teach classes – but you also need someone to manage the group's expenses, someone to take notes at group meetings, and someone to manage any website, social media pages, or private networks the group has. These more mundane jobs are essential in keeping the group running smoothly.

Think about what you and the other founders have planned for the group's future, then make a list of all the different jobs that will need to be done to make it happen. For example, if you are starting a teaching group, you'll need someone to write the curriculum, someone to teach the classes, someone to find a physical place to host classes in, someone to register students, and someone to advertise the classes on offer. While this could technically all be done by one person, it will be less overwhelming if the tasks are divided between several people.

Once you have a list of all the jobs that need to be done, go down the list and think about who in your group would be a good fit for each role. Think about who is willing to do the job and about who has the skills to do it well.

Going back to our teaching group example, you might have one member who has a very impressive understanding of the theory and practice of magic and is great at explaining it to others, but hates public speaking. Maybe that person could write the curriculum for your class and another member could do the teaching. Work with your members' strengths and preferences. Never force someone to do something they don't want to do or don't feel prepared for.

One of the roles you assign will probably be advertising the group. Advertising is how you get the word out so the world knows your group exists. If you plan to accept new members, advertising is absolutely essential.

I want to make a note that advertising is not the same as proselytizing. *Advertising* means simply telling people your group exists. *Proselytizing* means trying to make someone convert from one belief system to another, which is unethical and in poor taste.

When you advertise your group, you are simply spreading the word and hoping to reach other witchy types who might be interested in joining. You're saying, "Hey, we're here, we're doing our thing, and you're welcome to join us if you want to." When you proselytize, you put pressure on people to join up, even if they aren't interested. Proselytizing says, "Hey, I'm right and you're wrong, so you better quit what you're doing and start doing what I'm doing."

Proselytizing includes obvious methods like preaching or even explicitly telling someone that their beliefs are wrong, but it also includes more subtle manipulation. This includes practices like offering free meals to people in need, but only if they attend a class or spiritual service. It includes targeting children and teaching them about your own spiritual beliefs without their caretakers' consent. It includes focusing your recruitment efforts on people who are vulnerable, like recovering addicts or recent divorcees, and other underhanded methods of getting people to join up.

Witches do not proselytize. Make sure your advertisements stay lighthearted, approachable, and non-intrusive. Avoid anything that could come across as preachy or pushy.

Where and how you advertise depends on whether your group is in person or online. For an in-person group, you'll want to focus your advertising efforts in your local area. Look for the witch-friendly spots we mentioned in the "Finding a Group" section, like metaphysical stores, Pagan Pride festivals, and interfaith councils. Ask the owners or managers of these spaces if you can put up flyers, leave information cards, or tape a QR code in their window. You might also consider doing the same in local queer spaces like PFLAG meetings, Pride planning committees, drag shows, etc.

For an online group, you'll want to focus your advertising efforts online. The best place to start is by making social media pages for your group that will be visible to the public. Share a little bit of information about what your group does and who can join. If at all possible, include an eye-catching photo or video. Make a post on your social pages announcing that you're accepting new members. Depending on your group's budget, you might consider creating a paid advertisement on social apps like Facebook or Instagram.

Whether you are advertising in person or online, good design is key to creating advertisements that draw people in. A colorful flyer with beautiful illustrations and bold, easy-to-read text will get more attention than a plain, boring flyer. If anyone in your group is an experienced artist or graphic designer, this is a great role for them.

I use a website called Canva (www.canva.com) to create advertisements and graphics. Canva has ready-made templates that can be customized for your needs, and they have lots of great free assets. They also have a paid service, but you can get everything you need from the free version. Programs like Adobe InDesign and Photoshop are also an option.

You can also create posters, flyers, and business cards by hand if you are so inclined. If you or a member of your group enjoys making physical art, you can create a master copy of the advertisement by hand, then make copies to hang up as fliers or pass out as info cards. Physical art can be scanned and uploaded to a computer to be incorporated into social media graphics.

If your advertising is successful, you will start to connect with people who are interested in joining your group. It's important to have a screening process for new members.

The point of screening new members isn't to exclude people. Instead, the goal is to catch dangerous or bigoted people before they join so that they don't cause problems later. I want to stress that this process should only be used to deny entry to people if you have reason to believe they will cause serious physical or mental/emotional harm to members of your community.

If someone shows up to a group meeting with a visible swastika tattoo or a T-shirt that has a slur written on it, you probably don't want them in your group, for the safety of yourself and the other members. However, not all bad actors make themselves so obvious, which is why it's important to have a screening process in place.

Your screening process might start with an online questionnaire asking people a few questions about their interest in witchcraft and any previous magic experience. It might start with a member of your group's leadership meeting them to discuss their interest over coffee. It might start with a text message conversation where you invite them to ask questions and ask them to share a little about themself. Think about what a realistic and practical screening process looks like for your group.

One good way to weed out bigots is to ask newcomers if they belong to any other spiritual or religious groups. Write down the names of any groups they claim to be a member of and look those groups up later. If someone is a member of a tradition that has ties to white supremacist groups or that excludes transgender people from rituals, for example, they probably aren't someone you want in your community.

It's also a good idea to go through your group agreement with them and ask if they have any questions or concerns. If they disagree with your group's values or ask about exceptions to your non-discrimination policy, proceed with caution.

As we are screening new members, it is important for us to remember that no one is perfect. Just because someone isn't a perfect ally doesn't mean they're a bad person. They may want to do better and just need an opportunity to learn.

Even if someone doesn't share our politics, doesn't know the vocabulary, and has never done work as a queer ally before, they still have a place in our community as long as they share our values and agree to uphold our group agreement. If we only opened our doors to perfect allies, our communities would be very small indeed.

Once someone passes your screening process, invite them to attend a few events so they can get a feel for your group and decide if they want to join. During this time, be open to questions about your group and answer as honestly as possible. You may even want to have a designated welcome committee whose job is to make sure visitors feel included.

Make sure it is clear that visitors are free to leave at any time and that they are under no obligation to join if they don't want to. Sometimes a great person and a great group just aren't a good fit for each other, and it isn't anyone's fault. Thank them for their interest and let them go on friendly terms.

If someone has attended several events as a visitor but hasn't yet decided whether to join, it may be helpful for an experienced group member to talk to them privately about their decision. They can start by reminding the visitor that they are under no pressure to join, then ask if they have any questions or concerns they would like to discuss. The conversation should be friendly and supportive. This makes sure the visitor feels seen and valued.

In a perfect world, we would be able to focus on running our groups, welcoming new members, and enjoying the safe, affirming spaces we've created. Unfortunately, we do not live in a perfect world. In any group that goes on long enough, there will eventually be a member who behaves in inappropriate or harmful ways.

To save yourself some grief, make sure you have a process for dealing with problematic group members before you need it. In the early days of your group, all members should decide on this process together through voting or consensus.

When I say "problematic group members," I am talking about people who break the group agreement, harm or harass another group member, or do something to make another person in the group feel unsafe. These are not petty disagreements – these are serious threats to the stability and safety of your community, and they need to be taken seriously.

For example, let's say a member of your group makes a transphobic comment during a group event. Your group has several transgender members, some of whom were in the room when the comment was made. One of them shares with you that the comment made her feel unsafe in the group. How is the group going to respond?

If this is the person's first offense, it can be helpful to consider *calling in* before *calling out*. When I worked as a student work supervisor in a university setting, we used "calling out" and "calling in" to discuss different ways to address harmful behavior. When you *call someone out*, you bring public attention to the harm they've caused and demand a change in front of witnesses. When you *call someone in*, you bring them into a private conversation where you let them know why what they did was harmful and ask them to commit to making amends. Both calling in and calling out have a time and a place.

If someone's behavior is dangerous or abusive, a call out may be the safest and most effective way to confront them, especially if they have hurt multiple people in the group. However, calling out tends to make the person being called out feel defensive, which may make them double down. On the other hand, calling in gives people a chance to correct their actions without a public scandal, which may make them more willing to improve.

If you believe the harm someone caused was accidental or if you think they might be willing to change their ways, I recommend calling in before calling out. If the behavior was aggressive, intentional, or needs to be dealt with immediately, calling out may be necessary.

In the above example, you might talk to the other members of your group's leadership team and decide to call in the person who made the transphobic comment. You might arrange for two or three leaders to meet with the person who made the comment in a public place for a private conversation. At the same time, you might arrange for other leaders to check in on your group's transgender members and offer support.

You might start your conversation with the person who made the transphobic comment by asking them if they realize that what they said was offensive. It's possible they didn't realize the implication of what they were saying or were just repeating something they read online or heard on the news. If they do not understand why their comment was offensive, you can explain how they have hurt several members of the group. You might also remind them of your group agreement and non-discrimination statement.

At this point, the conversation will probably go one of two ways. Either this person will feel remorse for the harm they caused and will commit to doing better, or they will double down and refuse to change.

In our example, if the person who made the transphobic comment is remorseful, you could offer them some resources to help them be a better ally and ask them to apologize to your group's trans members. If they double down, you could calmly and professionally inform them that if they are not willing to uphold the group agreement, they are no longer welcome in the group.

Remember, as queer people, it is not our job to educate others about gender and sexuality. If someone says or does something queerphobic, we do not owe them a second chance. We have to think about our own safety and the safety of our community above all else.

References and Bibliography

Ahlquist, D. (2017). *Moon Magic: Your Complete Guide to Harnessing the Mystical Energy of the Moon*. Simon and Schuster.

Ainsworth, C. (2018, October 22). *Sex Redefined: The idea of 2 sexes is overly simplistic*. Scientific American. https://www.scientificamerican.com/article/sex-redefined-the-idea-of-2-sexes-is-overly-simplistic1/

Animism. (2023). In *Merriam-Webster Dictionary*. https://www.merriam-webster.com/dictionary/animsm

Auryn, M. (2018). The Blue God Of Faery. *For Puck's Sake*. https://www.patheos.com/blogs/matauryn/2018/07/31/blue-god-faery/

Bartlett, R. A. (2009). *Real Alchemy: A Primer of Practical Alchemy*. Nicolas-Hays, Inc.

BBC News. (2022, November 22). *Club Q Colorado shooting: Attack was ended by dad and show performer*. https://www.bbc.com/news/world-us-canada-63698165

Betancourt, R. (2020, October 7). The overlooked queer history of medieval Christianity. *Time*. https://time.com/5896685/queer-monks-medieval-history/

Cartwright, M. (2023). Izanami and Izanagi. *World History Encyclopedia*. https://www.worldhistory.org/Izanami_and_Izanagi/

Chamberlain, L. (2014). *Wicca Elemental Magic: A Guide to the Elements, Witchcraft, and Magic Spells*. Createspace Independent Publishing Platform.

Chamberlain, L. (2016). *Wicca Moon Magic: A Wiccan's Guide and Grimoire for Working Magic with Lunar Energies*. Createspace Independent Publishing Platform.

Clauss, J. J., & Johnston, S. I. (Eds.). (1997). *Medea: Essays on Medea in Myth, Literature, Philosophy, and Art*. Princeton University Press. https://doi.org/10.2307/j.ctv10vm25j

Conner, R. P. L. (2000). Men-Women, Gatekeepers, and Fairy Mounds. *Parabola,* 25(1), 71-77.

Crawford, J. (2019). *The Wanderer's Havamal*. Hackett Publishing.

Cunningham, S. (2011). *Cunningham's Encyclopedia of Crystal, Gem & Metal Magic*. Llewellyn Worldwide.

Cunningham, S. (2012). *Cunningham's Encyclopedia of Magical Herbs*. Llewellyn Worldwide.

Cunningham, S. (2004). *Wicca: A Guide for the Solitary Practitioner*. Llewellyn Publications.

Daimler, M. (2013). *Where the Hawthorn Grows: An American Druid's Reflections.* Moon Books.

Dorsey, L. (2020). *Orishas, Goddesses, and Voodoo Queens: The Divine Feminine in the African Religious Traditions*. Adfo Books.

Duberman, M. (2019). *Stonewall: The Definitive Story of the LGBT Rights Uprising that Changed America*. Penguin.

Farrar, J., & Farrar, S. (1989). *The Witches' God*. Phoenix Publishing Inc.

Farrar, J., & Farrar, S. (1987). *The Witches' Goddess*. Phoenix Publishing Inc.

GLAAD. (2023, May 1). *LGBTQ Community Calendar GLAAD*. GLAAD | GLAAD. https://glaad.org/reference/calendar/

Goodman, E. (2019, June 19). How the Lavender Menace Fought for Lesbian Liberation in the 1970s. *Them*. https://www.them.us/story/lavender-menace

Grossman, P. (2020). *Waking the Witch: Reflections on Women, Magic, and Power* (Reprint). Gallery Books.

Halley, C. (2020). Four flowering plants that have been decidedly queered. *JSTOR Daily*. https://daily.jstor.org/four-flowering-plants-decidedly-queered/

Haupt, L. L. (2021). *Rooted: Life at the Crossroads of Science, Nature, and Spirit*. Hachette UK.

Heath, C. (2021). *Elves, Witches & Gods: Spinning Old Heathen Magic in the Modern Day*. Llewellyn Publications.

Heliogabalus' religion (1) – Livius. (n.d.). https://www.livius.org/articles/person/heliogabalus/heliogabalus-religion-1/?

Human Rights Campaign. (2020, November 23). *Two spirit and LGBTQ identities: Today and centuries ago – HRC*. Human Rights Campaign. https://www.hrc.org/news/two-spirit-and-lgbtq-idenitites-today-and-centuries-ago

Johns, A. (2004). *Baba Yaga: the ambiguous mother and witch of the Russian folktale* (Ser. International folkloristics, vol. 3). Lang.

Johnston, E. (2023, October 23). *Four flowers that have become queer symbols*. Kew. Retrieved January 29, 2025, from https://www.kew.org/read-and-watch/plants-LGBTQ-symbols

Kahn, E. (n.d.). *Lavender menace action at Second Congress to Unite Women – NYC LGBT Historic Sites Project*. NYC LGBT Historic Sites Project. Retrieved January 29, 2025, from https://www.nyclgbtsites.org/site/lavender-menace-action-at-second-congress-to-unite-women/

Kent, A. E. (2016). *The Essential Guide to Practical Astrology: Everything from Zodiac Signs to Prediction, Made Easy and Entertaining*. Two Moon Publishing.

Kimmerer, R. W. (2020). *Braiding Sweetgrass: Indigenous Wisdom, Scientific Knowledge and the Teachings of Plants*. Penguin UK.

Knightly, Z. H. (2021, June 11). *The LGBTQ+ Reclamation of "Ergi" in Norse Heathenry*. Skald's Keep. https://skaldskeep.com/the-lgbtq-reclamation-of-ergi-in-norse-heathenry/

Leaver, S. (2021). *Hellenic Paganism.* Moon Books.

Le Guin, U. K. (2012). *A Wizard Of Earthsea*. HarperCollins.

Le Guin, U. K. (2019). *Lao Tzu: Tao Te Ching: A Book about the Way and the Power of the Way*. Shambhala Publications.

Liberman, A. (2015, July 30). *The Oxford Etymologist goes Trick-or-Treating*. OUPblog. https://blog.oup.com/2007/10/witch/

Liminal. (2023). In *The Merriam-Webster.com Dictionary*. https://www.merriam-webster.com/dictionary/liminal

Luu, T. (2021, December 21). *Queer Botany: The Sapphic Violet*. University of Washington Botanic Gardens. Retrieved

January 29, 2025, from https://botanicgardens.uw.edu/about/blog/2021/12/21/queer-botany-the-sapphic-violet/

March, L. (2021). Queer and trans* geographies of liminality: A literature review. *Progress in Human Geography,* 45(3), 455–471. https://doi.org/10.1177/0309132520913111

Martin, D. (2015). *A Green Witch's Cupboard.*

McMillan, K. (n.d.). *Violet delights: A queer history of purple.* V&A Dundee. Retrieved January 29, 2025, from https://www.vam.ac.uk/dundee/articles/violet-delights-a-queer-history-of-purple?srsltid=AfmBOoqZMTxSnLaAkoHOVCIL9UdNlcqUlKzG6KnJCFElZgTIyhpMlgP6

Medhurst, E. (2024, October 1). *From Lavender to Violet: The Lesbian Obsession with Purple.* Dressing Dykes. Retrieved January 29, 2025, from https://dressingdykes.com/2021/08/20/from-lavender-to-violet/

Morningbird. (2023, March 2). Planet Mars: Astrology, Associations, Healing & Magick. *Magickal Spot.* https://magickalspot.com/mars/

Morningbird. (2023, March 1). Planet Mercury: Correspondences, Magick & Astrology. *Magickal Spot.* https://magickalspot.com/mercury/

Morningbird. (2023, March 2). Planet Neptune: Key Correspondences & Associations. *Magickal Spot.* https://magickalspot.com/neptune/

Morningbird. (2023, March 15). Planet Jupiter: Correspondences, Magick & Astrology. *Magickal Spot.* https://magickalspot.com/jupiter-planet/

Morningbird. (2023, March 13). Planet Saturn: Correspondences, Magick & Astrology. *Magickal Spot.* https://magickalspot.com/saturn/

Morningbird. (2023, March 13). Planet Venus: Astrology, Associations & Magick. *Magickal Spot.* https://magickalspot.com/venus/

Morningbird. (2023, March 13). Sun: Astrology, Deities, Correspondences & Magick. *Magickal Spot*. https://magickalspot.com/sun/

Morrison, D. (2012). *Everyday Sun Magic: Spells & Rituals for Radiant Living*. Llewellyn Worldwide.

Nashville Tree Conservation Corps. (2022). Transsexual trees: Can trees change gender? *Nashville Tree Conservation Corps*. https://www.nashvilletreeconservationcorps.org/treenews/transsexual-trees-can-trees-change-gender

Naydler, J. (1996). *Temple of the Cosmos: The Ancient Egyptian Experience of the Sacred*. Inner Traditions.

Oberon, A. (2019). *Southern Cunning: Folkloric Witchcraft In The American South*. Moon Books.

Ogles, J. (2017, November 6). 15 LGBT Egyptian Gods. *Advocate.com*. https://www.advocate.com/arts-entertainment/2016/9/20/15-lgbt-egyptian-gods

Orr, E. R. (2012). *The Wakeful World: Animism, Mind and the Self in Nature*. Moon Books.

Pagliarulo, A. (2022, October 30). Why paganism and witchcraft are making a comeback. *NBC News*. Retrieved September 18, 2023, from https://www.nbcnews.com/think/opinion/paganism-witchcraft-are-making-comeback-rcna54444

Patterson, R. (2019). *Pagan Portals – Sun Magic: How To Live In Harmony With The Solar Year*. Moon Books.

PBS NewsHour. (2022, November 27). *Club Q patron who helped stop shooter said he 'wanted to save the family I found.'* https://www.pbs.org/newshour/nation/club-q-patron-who-helped-stop-shooter-said-he-wanted-to-save-the-family-i-found

Reed, T. (2019). *Astrology for real life: A Workbook for Beginners*. Weiser Books.

Riske, K. B. (2010). *Llewellyn's Complete Book of Astrology: The Easy Way to Learn Astrology*. Llewellyn Worldwide.

Sabin, T. (2006). *Wicca for Beginners: Fundamentals of Philosophy & Practice*. Llewellyn Worldwide Limited.

Scharping, N. (2019). Why this fungus has over 20,000 sexes. *Discover Magazine*. https://www.discovermagazine.com/planet-earth/why-this-fungus-has-over-20-000-sexes

Schrefer, E. (2023). *Queer ducks (and other animals): The Natural World of Animal Sexuality*. Katherine Tegen Books.

Siobhan. (2017). Let's Talk About Dionysus, Genderqueer God of Partying and Pride. *Autostraddle*. https://www.autostraddle.com/lets-talk-about-dionysus-genderqueer-god-of-partying-and-pride-379653/

Smith, R. (2019). *The Way of Fire and Ice: The Living Tradition of Norse Paganism*. Llewellyn.

Snow, C. (2020). *Queering Your Craft: Witchcraft from the Margins*. Weiser Books.

Sollée, K. J. (2017). *Witches, Sluts, Feminists: Conjuring the Sex Positive*. ThreeL Media.

Starhawk. (1999). *The Spiral Dance: a rebirth of the ancient religion of the Great Goddess* (20th Anniversary). HarperOne.

Starr, Lilith. (2021). *Compassionate Satanism: An Introduction to Modern Satanic Practice*. Lilith Starr Studios.

Sy, S., & Dubnow, S. (2024, March 14). What Florida's "Don't Say Gay" settlement changes and what restrictions remain. *PBS News*. https://www.pbs.org/newshour/show/what-floridas-dont-say-gay-settlement-changes-and-what-restrictions-remain

Teish, L. (2021). *Jambalaya: The Natural Woman's Book of Personal Charms and Practical Rituals*. HarperCollins.

Tourjée, D. (2017, October 4). Yes, There Are Trans Animals. *Vice*. Retrieved July 18, 2023, from https://www.vice.com/en/article/8x8bez/yes-there-are-trans-animals

Valiente, Doreen. *Charge of the Goddess*. Accessed via the Doreen Valiente Foundation. https://www.doreenvaliente.com/doreen-valiente-Doreen_Valiente_Poetry-11.php

Wigington, P. (2019, November 13). *Februalia: a time of purification*. Learn Religions. https://www.learnreligions.com/the-roman-februalia-festival-2562114

Wigington, P. "What Is the Wiccan Rede?" *Learn Religions*, Learn Religions, 23 Dec. 2018, https://www.learnreligions.com/the-wiccan-rede-2562601.

Witch. (2023). In *The Merriam-Webster.com Dictionary*. https://www.merriam-webster.com/dictionary/witch

Woolfold, J. M. (2008). *The Only Astrology Book You'll Ever Need*. Taylor Trade Publications.

Zakroff, L. T. (2019). *Weave the Liminal: Living Modern Traditional Witchcraft*. Llewellyn Publications.

Zhang, Yuxin. (2015, June 22). China's misunderstood history of gay tolerance. *The Diplomat*. https://thediplomat.com/2015/06/chinas-misunderstood-history-of-gay-tolerance/

MOON BOOKS

PAGANISM & SHAMANISM

What is Paganism? A religion, a spirituality, an alternative belief system, nature worship? You can find support for all these definitions (and many more) in dictionaries, encyclopaedias, and text books of religion, but subscribe to any one and the truth will evade you. Above all Paganism is a creative pursuit, an encounter with reality, an exploration of meaning and an expression of the soul. Druids, Heathens, Wiccans and others, all contribute their insights and literary riches to the Pagan tradition. Moon Books invites you to begin or to deepen your own encounter, right here, right now.

If you have enjoyed this book, why not tell other readers by posting a review on your preferred book site.

Bestsellers from Moon Books

Keeping Her Keys
An Introduction to Hekate's Modern Witchcraft
Cyndi Brannen
Blending Hekate, witchcraft and personal development together to create a powerful new magickal perspective.
Paperback: 978-1-78904-075-3 ebook 978-1-78904-076-0

Journey to the Dark Goddess
How to Return to Your Soul
Jane Meredith
Discover the powerful secrets of the Dark Goddess and transform your depression, grief and pain into healing and integration.
Paperback: 978-1-84694-677-6 ebook: 978-1-78099-223-5

Shamanic Reiki
Expanded Ways of Working with Universal Life Force Energy
Llyn Roberts, Robert Levy
Shamanism and Reiki are each powerful ways of healing; together, their power multiplies. Shamanic Reiki introduces techniques to help healers and Reiki practitioners tap ancient healing wisdom.
Paperback: 978-1-84694-037-8 ebook: 978-1-84694-650-9

Southern Cunning
Folkloric Witchcraft in the American South
Aaron Oberon
Modern witchcraft with a Southern flair, this book is a journey through the folklore of the American South and a look at the power these stories hold for modern witches.
Paperback: 978-1-78904-196-5 ebook: 978-1-78904-197-2

Bestsellers from Moon Books
Pagan Portals Series

The Morrigan

Meeting the Great Queens

Morgan Daimler

Ancient and enigmatic, the Morrigan reaches out to us. On shadowed wings and in raven's call, meet the ancient Irish goddess of war, battle, prophecy, death, sovereignty, and magic.

Paperback: 978-1-78279-833-0 ebook: 978-1-78279-834-7

The Awen Alone

Walking the Path of the Solitary Druid

Joanna van der Hoeven

An introductory guide for the solitary Druid, The Awen Alone will accompany you as you explore, and seek out your own place within the natural world.

Paperback: 978-1-78279-547-6 ebook: 978-1-78279-546-9

Moon Magic

Rachel Patterson

An introduction to working with the phases of the Moon, what they are and how to live in harmony with the lunar year and to utilise all the magical powers it provides.

Paperback: 978-1-78279-281-9 ebook: 978-1-78279-282-6

Hekate

A Devotional

Vivienne Moss

Hekate, Queen of Witches and the Shadow-Lands, haunts the pages of this devotional bringing magic and enchantment into your lives.

Paperback: 978-1-78535-161-7 ebook: 978-1-78535-162-4

Readers of ebooks can buy or view any of these bestsellers by clicking on the live link in the title. Most titles are published in paperback and as an ebook. Paperbacks are available in traditional bookshops. Both print and ebook formats are available online.

Find more titles and sign up to our readers' newsletter
www.collectiveinkbooks.com/paganism

YouTube

For video content, author interviews and more, please subscribe to our YouTube channel.

MoonBooksPublishing

Follow us on social media for book news, promotions and more:

Facebook: Moon Books

Instagram: @MoonBooksCI

X: @MoonBooksCI X: @MoonBooksCI

Bluesky: moonbooksci.bsky.social

TikTok: @MoonBooksCI